TOM SHIELDS' DIARY

Tom Shields was born in Glasgow in 1948 and has never really left the place since. He was educated at Lourdes Secondary but there was no miracle. He very nearly became a mathematician at Strathclyde University. He has worked as a journalist at the *Glasgow Herald* since 1973.

TOM SHIELDS' DIARY

TOM SHIELDS

MAINSTREAM
PUBLISHING
EDINBURGH AND LONDON

First published in Great Britain 1991 by
MAINSTREAM PUBLISHING COMPANY (EDINBURGH) LTD
7 Albany Street
Edinburgh EH1 3UG

ISBN 1 85158 491 9

A catalogue record for this book is available from the British Library

Typeset in Plantin by SX Composing Ltd, Essex

Printed in Great Britain by Butler & Tanner Ltd, Frome

CONTENTS

PREFACE

IF I were to thank by name all of the people who have helped me to write the *Herald* Diary in the past 12 years, this acknowledgment would be longer than the text of the book. The Diary belongs to its readers, contributors, critics, and friends. I am grateful to them, one and all. I am merely the chap who opens the mail, writes up the *bons mots*, takes the credit when it is going, and goes into hiding when the going gets tough.

This book is dedicated to Arnold Kemp, Harry Reid and Ron Anderson – my three superior officers. Three exceptional editors who have created an atmosphere which allows the Diary to thrive.

Tom Shields
Glasgow, 1991

FOREWORD

MOST people who read the *Glasgow Herald* will agree that the Tom Shields Diary has become an institution. And not a few outside the circle may consider that its author and devotees should perhaps be incarcerated in one.

However, aficionados/as, not to mention people who enjoy it, will rejoice that the best of the Diary has at last been encapsulated between the covers of this unique volume. Not since Mr Samuel Pepys's assiduous assessment of antiquity has there been such a valuable documentation of our life and times, and this book will doubtless, in due course, become the bible of historians, not to mention students of etymology and dirty-talk.

Indeed, with such importance is it regarded in scholarly circles, that there are calls for a new time-capsule to be buried beneath the medical centre complex being built at Clydebank, which will contain not only the Diary, but also the Scottish National Party's Election manifesto, Neil Kinnock's shorter speeches (24 volumes), Ron Brown's memoirs and a Motherwell District Councillor. In this way it is hoped that future generations can have a good laugh as well.

Here, thankfully, not only for posterity but for now and the immediate future, is the item that caused the coffee spill at breakfast that morning, or the soft-boiled egg to explode over the wean. Or the one which kept you laughing even as you got on the bus and sat down on top of that big wumman. Here, thankfully, is the granting of the oft-repeated wish that you had kept the cuttings over the years.

'I never travel without my diary.
One should always have something
sensational to read in the train.'
Oscar Wilde, 1854-1900

Read and enjoy, compadres. All is now right with the world. God's in His heaven, and the Diary is in print.

Rikki Fulton
Glasgow 1991

APOCRYPHA

There is an old saying in the Diary business that certain stories are too good to check out. Unfortunately, this is not true. The libel laws prohibit such a luxury. But occasionally, once we have tried manfully to establish the truth of a story and failed, we still print it, with no names, on the grounds that it will do no one any harm:

A WOMAN is driving home from her work at Glasgow Airport. Some way along the M8, she spots a microwave oven lying on the verge. She stops and stows the oven in the boot of her car. She drives off but only gets a few hundred yards along the motorway when she is pulled into the side by a police car. The police tell her not to worry but could they have their speed-testing device back, please?

THE average Scot's lack of foreign languages is highlighted in this little tale of a chap who went on a Mediterranean cruise. Being on his own, he was asked if he would mind sharing a dinner table with another passenger, a Frenchman, who was also travelling alone. The Frenchman spoke no English and the Scotsman, a Mr Bob Speirs, spoke no French.

At the first meal, the French chap said 'Bon appetit' to which the Scot replied 'Bob Speirs'. At the second and third meals the Frenchman said 'Bon appetit' to which the Scot replied 'Bob Speirs'.

The ship's purser asked Mr Speirs how he was getting on with his table companion. 'He's a friendly enough chap,' Speirs replied, 'but he keeps forgetting we've met and keeps introducing himself as Bon Appetit.'

The purser explained that this was French for 'enjoy your meal'.

Thus clued up, Mr Speirs greeted the Frenchman at the next meal with the words 'Bon appetit'. The Frenchman smiled and replied: 'Bob Speirs.'

THIS story is supposed to have happened at the Brixton riots, but we cannot believe this of our boys in blue.

A young PC has lost his nerve and run away from the bricks and petrol bombs of the front line. He is taking shelter, head in hands, in a shop doorway. Next thing he sees is a pair of well-polished boots. A voice booms out that he should be ashamed of himself. He has let the force, and himself, down.

'I'm sorry, sergeant,' he says without looking up.

'What do you mean "sergeant". I'm an inspector.'

To which the PC replied: 'I'm sorry, sir. I didn't think I'd retreated that far.'

AN apprentice joiner called in to fix a neighbour's pulley as a favour.

Having completed the work, he went through to the parlour and said to the woman: 'That's your pulley fixed, Mrs Brown. Noo ye can get yer claes up.'

The lady, taken aback, said: 'Well, OK, but I was just going to give you a bottle of whisky.'

THE Diary credited this story to Sydney Devine but we subsequently heard it attributed to Andy Cameron and other radio presenters who deal with children's jokes, so it has to go under the heading of apocryphal.

A wee boy contacts the phone-in with the query: 'What vegetable brings tears to your eyes?'

No, the answer was not an onion. Nor was it any other potentially nippy veg which the presenter suggested. So, which vegetable brings tears to your eyes?

'A turnip,' said the wee boy.

A turnip? 'Aye, if you get hit in the ba's wi' a turnip, it brings tears to your eyes,' quoth the urchin.

SIGN in Ayrshire pub: 'Welcome – A Pint, a Pie, and a Kind Word.' A visitor duly followed the suggestion on the sign. The barmaid slammed his pint in front of him without a word. She was equally taciturn when she dumped an extremely greasy and aged pie on the bar.

'What about the kind word?' he asked.

'Don't eat the pie,' she retorted.

A GLASGOW housewife emptied her shopping on to the kitchen table. Returning minutes later she discovered that a pack of Penguin biscuits had been opened and two taken.

'Ye wee scoundrel' (or words to that effect), she said. 'Ah'll get the polis tae ye.'

Ten minutes later, as the urchin played outside, a police constable (in pursuit of other inquiries) approached the close-mouth. Anxious to get his version in first, the boy stopped the PC with the words: 'It wasnae me that stole the chocolate biscuits. And anyway that old bitch doesnae huv a TV licence.'

THIS is the story of an embarrassing encounter between an Ayrshire doctor and a young married woman patient.

The woman, whose husband had been away at sea for some time, was lying back on the doctor's couch for an intimate examination. Just as the GP was about to begin, the woman said: 'You'll have to do something about the cobwebs.'

The GP, slightly puzzled by the remark and assuming it was a reference to the long time her sailor husband had been away, replied: 'I'll leave that for your husband to deal with.'

The woman, having recovered from a severe fit of the giggles, explained that she was referring to the cobwebs on the ceiling of his surgery.

THIS story is supposed to have happened at a wedding, deep in the heart of a small North-east farming community.

After a charming church service and at the end of a traditional wedding party, the bridegroom stood up to make a wee speech. Having thanked the bride's parents for a wonderful spread, he said, 'Now, at this point, my wife and I should be heading off for our honeymoon. In fact, I have the tickets here for the holiday in the sun,' and produced the travel documents from his inside pocket. 'But I think it's more appropriate that the best man should take them. After all, he's been sleeping with my wife for the past six months!'

A GROUP of executives from a top Japanese car firm were in Gleneagles Hotel for a conference.

They had ordered full Highland dress and the six were making their way down the grand staircase for dinner when horror-struck staff noticed they were all wearing their kilts back to front. Sporrans, kilt pins, pleats – the lot – were facing backwards.

Experts in sorting out just about every situation, the loyal staff stepped in, erected a makeshift screen of towels and, right there in the foyer, turned the backside-foremost garments round with a resounding 'wheech'.

It is reliably reported that the Japanese delegation returned home with tales of the marvellous Scottish customs which are associated with the wearing of the kilt.

It is not known whether anything was worn under the kilt on this occasion or whether everything was in perfect working order.

THE City of Culture celebrations gave rein to Glasgow's talent for xeno-phobia. Hence the tale of the German visitor to the city who witnessed a Glasgow wummin skelping her wean in Central Station.

The German reproached the woman saying: 'In Germany we do not hit our children.'

'Is that right?' the woman replied. 'In Partick we don't gas Jews.'

THEN there was the following exchange:

Japanese Tourist: 'Excuse me, can you direct me to George Square?'
Glesca Keelie: 'You found Pearl Harbour easily enough. Find George Square your f★★★★★★ self.'

AN Edinburgh couple had to move to Glasgow because of the husband's job. In the Glasgow way, the couple were quickly befriended by the wummin next door.

Now, it was this Edinburgh lady's custom of a morning to entertain a gentleman friend. One morning in the course of the entertainment, the chap suffered a heart attack and died.

Distraught, the lady consulted her neighbour for advice. After only a few moments of thought, the Glasgow woman said: 'Nae problem, hen, jist stick a shammy in his haun' and drap him oot the windae.'

THIS conversation, overheard at the Plaza Ballroom, is hopefully apocryphal.

Two young ladies exiting from toilets.

One says: 'Senga, d'you know you've got a Tampax behind your ear?'

To which Senga replies: 'Oh, Goad, what huv ah done wi' ma fag?'

OF similar nature is the tale of a doctor whose colleague remarks: 'Do you know you've got a suppository behind your ear?'

'Is that right?' the doctor replies. 'In that case whit erse has goat ma pencil?'

Here comes his wife back from the shops. She spots the legs sticking out from under the car. Being in a mischievous mood, she gives a tweak – a friendly but firm tweak – just where the legs of the dungarees meet.

Then she walks into the kitchen to find her husband making a cup of tea. And in walks a mechanic from the local garage with blood pouring from the wound suffered when his head suddenly and involuntarily hit the underside of the car.

THIS is supposed to have happened to a burgher of Hamilton. There he is, in his dungarees, under the car doing a spot of vehicular DIY. His wife pops off to the shops.

OFFICE parties are a fertile source of apocryphal stories. This one involved a young lady, usually of impeccable behaviour, at a British Telecom staffie in Glasgow.

15

She had taken too much drink and was poured into a taxi. At her destination, she made her way unsteadily up the path. When her father opened the door, she began to apologise profusely, if slightly incoherently.

Her dad, a man of the world, told her not to worry, come in, have a cup of coffee. 'Anyway, you don't have to apologise to me,' he explained. 'You seem to have forgotten you don't live here anymore. You got married three months ago.'

THEN there was the tale of the man who woke up with a black eye the morning after the office party.

'I'm sorry, dear,' he told his darling wife, 'I don't know how I came home with this black eye.'

'That's all right, dear,' she replied, 'You got it after you came home.'

ANOTHER husband, returning in a terrible state at 4 a.m., so infuriated his wife that she threw the alarm clock at him. As his colleagues remarked the next day: 'It's amazing how time flies when you're enjoying yourself.'

AS ITHERS SEE US

As part of a long-term quest 'Tae See Oorsels as Ithers See Us', the Diary monitored publications from England and many other foreign countries:

GLASGOW University football team, on tour in the USA, visited Wheaton College near Chicago, the Bible-thumping alma mater of Billy Graham. The Glasgow chaps detected a certain reserve in the attitude of their American hosts. This, they discovered, was down to a circular letter which the college had distributed to their students, on the subject of the Glasgow Yooni team: 'Please keep in mind that these young men are not Christians. We have a great opportunity to share our lifestyle and Christian principles with them.

'All of them are drinkers! They have been briefed on Wheaton's standards and the non-drinking procedures. Please be firm in reminding them of this, because they may try to bring their own drinks into your home.'

The Glasgow players, a bunch of red-blooded young men who liked the occasional lager, had to observe a strict 11 p.m. curfew. The two unlucky enough to be billeted with the college team coach had to get up at 5.30 a.m. for a cross-country run.

The Glaswegians did their best to cope with all this. But when a Wheatonite asked one of them: 'Do you really have no Christians in Scotland?' he replied: 'There were two or three, but we ate them.'

A JOURNALIST dispatched to Glasgow by the magazine *New Society* reported in February 1981: 'When I went to Glasgow last month I saw only two drunks.' The reason was not an outbreak of sobriety but the 'fact' that most Glaswegians could not afford the bus fares to visit the city centre.

17

The magazine also reported that Mr Fred Edwards, the city's 'restless and brilliant' social work director had gathered around him 'a team of SAS social workers' which was making 'creative blitzkriegs on community problems'. The magazine did not indicate if the brilliant Mr Edwards had any plans to sort out the bus fares crisis.

IN the same month, very much pre-Year of Culture status, a book called *An Australian's Guide to Britain* (which carried the imprimatur of British Airways) said of the city: 'Glasgow is not well supplied with good accommodation and in any case is not worthy of an overnight stay. However, a visit of a few hours will probably be judged worth while.'

AN advertisement for Dewar's whisky in American magazines caused some wry amusement among the inhabitants of the picturesque Fife village of Culross. Under a photograph of an old chap walking his collie dog through the cobbled streets of the village, ran the words: 'He was never elected. But every night "Mayor" Orlo McBain is the last man to walk the streets of Culross, Scotland. He checks a knob, closes a gate and goes his way. The good things in life stay that way.'

'Who is this Mayor Orlo McBain?' we asked the Culross police.

'Never heard of him,' the constable said. 'If anyone was wandering around late at night checking knobs and closing gates I'm sure we would have noticed. The only character we have ever had was a woman called Fanny Scotland who used to ring the town bell.'

The mystery was solved when Mr Ian McLeod, curator of the large number of National Trust for Scotland properties in Culross, revealed that he was the man in the picture. A team had arrived in the village from a Chicago advertising agency and asked him to pose with a borrowed collie dog.

Mr McLeod said of the Orlo McBain story: 'It is dreadful nonsense, but if it helps sell Scotch in the USA it might do some good.'

The National Trust received a $100 donation and the owner of the dog got $25. Presumably the writer of the advertisement copy also got to sample rather a lot of the product.

ANOTHER whisky company to go in for couthy Scots advertising around this time was Macallan. One of their ads told the tale of Alfred, a barman at the Caledonian Club in London who refused to allow a Texan visitor to put ginger ale into a measure of 15-year-old Macallan malt. Alfred was quoted as saying to the Texan: 'I'll no' be a party to defacing national monuments.' Of the Macallan, Alfred was reputed to have told the Texan: 'I doubt ye'll find better.'

We tracked down Alfred the barman at the Caledonian Club. He said 'It's all a bit embarrassing. I don't speak like that. In fact, no one does in Burton-on-

Trent where I come from. It was fun at the time but the joke is now wearing thin, especially since I only got one bottle of the stuff for letting them use my name.'

AS part of a national campaign, Castlemilk Law Centre, the only such centre in Scotland, wrote to Lord Hailsham, the Lord Chancellor, even though they knew he was not associated with the legal system in Scotland. The letter produced this response: 'Lord Hailsham is Lord Chancellor of Great Britain, which does not, as you know, include Scotland.'

IT is not only Sassenachs and other foreigners who can come up with a picture of Glasgow that is slightly agley. The organisers of an event called Welcome Home 1983 showed a little less than encyclopaedic knowledge of their own city by producing a list of famous Glaswegians including: Lord Kelvin, inventor of Bovril; Saint Kentigan (*sic*) who was burnt at the stake in 1582; Peter Kerrigan, patron saint of Glasgow; Harry Lauder, a tobacco merchant; Thomas Lipton, a famous socialist; Tam Harvey, the Glasgow glutton; and Madeleine Smith, 'famous murderer of the Boys' Brigade'.

The organisers blamed the historic gaffes on an errant word processor, a piece of kit not, as far as we know, invented by a Glaswegian.

Elspeth King, curator of the

People's Palace, was angered that the above list was somewhat short of female representation. She immediately came up with 18 names of notable Glaswegian women. It started off with St Thenew (or Enoch), mother of St Kentigern, patron saint of the city. In her inimitable style, Elspeth described St Thenew as 'Scotland's first fully documented battered woman, rape victim and unmarried mother'. Her list included a number of suffragettes, the Diary's favourite being one Elizabeth Dorothea Chalmers Smith, a well-known doctor whose suffragist principles led her to set fire to 6 Park Gardens on 24 July 1913.

No, Dr Smith was not ahead of her time in burning to the ground the HQ of the male chauvinist Scottish Football Association. The SFA did not move in until 1957. In 1913, the premises were occupied by the Lord Provost of Glasgow. Still, the thought was there.

MR Tony Benn, chairing a Labour Party public meeting in London, on economic strategy, declared that to make question time fair he would take questions alternately from men and women. The system worked well until there were no women left to put questions. With barely a pause, Mr Benn looked around the audience and asked: 'Is there anyone here from Scotland?' Presumably on the basis that in the absence of a woman, a man in a kilt will do.

19

A LEAFLET about Glasgow, produced for visitors to a Scottish Design Engineering Show held in the city, informed them: 'Heavy bombing has left much of Glasgow's publand derelict and very few of the original pubs remain.' The leaflet was produced by a company from Farnham, Surrey.

RALEIGH (Glasgow) Ltd, a whisky producer, received the following telex from a Norwegian student:

Dear Mr Raleigh,

In the late July my companion, Mr H. G. Toreskaas and myself are going on an expedition of studies to Scotland. The purpose of the expedition is primarily to study the different brands of Scottish whisky and secondly to make a pre-project for my master degree in anthropology, which will be a comparative study of sheep shepherds' working methods in Scotland and Norway, stressed on the threatening of wolves of lack of threatening? (How is the stock of wolves in Scotland?)

To carry through our expedition, we need a tandem bicycle (we have heard much about the extreme fog in England and due to that we must have a tandem so that we don't get lost for each other). We prefer to rent the tandem in Aberdeen. If that is unpossible we'll have to buy a tandem in Aberdeen. We would ask you to advice us a bicycle shop in Aberdeen where this is possible and return the address, telephone number and telex. Is it possible to get a price offer? a) for rent; b) for sale.

We thank you very much for your co-operation in advance, and your name will be listed in the honouring list in the preface of our report.

A KISSOGRAM agency in London offers a Drunken Scots service. The act consists of a male employee (usually a genuine Scot) who turns up in kilt, a funny hat, bloomers, clutching a can of beer and proceeds to be a drunk Jock. For an extra payment, the Jockogram will show what is worn under his kilt. Presumably for no extra charge he will deliver a Glasgow kiss.

Other national stereotypes offered by the agency? A blonde Swede or a witch doctor. If they had an English-o-gram it would no doubt be someone who would bore the party to death with details of traffic conditions during his journey.

THE magazine *New Society* carried a report on down-and-outs in London. Naturally, one of the interviewees was a Scot: 'Jimmy has the cheerful, child-like face of "Oor Wullie" from the Scottish cartoon strip.' Oor Jimmy goes on ('in a serious Dundee voice') to describe his drinking habits: 'I'm a very hard drinker. I'll drink anything. I had three bottles of aftershave and a bucket. I went out and got some hair lacquer. I put it all in the bucket and I drank it. I was staggering about bumping into walls. I was in the sick bay for three weeks.' No wonder Oor Wullie's hair stands on end if that's what Dundonians do with their buckets.

MUHAMMAD Mahfouz, correspondent of the *Saudi Gazette*, on a visit to Scotland provided an insight into that rare breed, the Highlander. The Highlanders, he said, 'live in the mountains, which is a rather forbidding zone, and a collection of islands in the north-west'. According to Muhammad, Highlanders are still fighting, and losing, the wars of 1715 and 1745. The Highlanders 'have a lot of tolerance for hardships. They have scorn for ordinary work and technical skills and love to fight, to drink, and to sail.'

THE annual report of the Commissioner for Local Administration in Scotland is a weighty tome, but it is not without its lighter moments. It records a letter from an inquiring student which said: 'I would be extremely grateful if you could send me information on the geography, climate, countryside, costumes, music, and national dancing of Scotland. If this isn't possible, could you please send me the address of the Scottish Embassy.' The student lives in England.

THE *Sunday Correspondent* newspaper of blessed memory contained a report about 'Glasgow's most frightening pub, the Saracen's Head, frequented by early-morning Barras workers. It is known as the Sarrie Heid (sore head) locally, because few people leave the establishment without one.'

The writer informed us further that it is 'easier to get a cappuccino in the city centre than it is to get a haggis supper (battered entrails and chips), such is the explosion of cafes and designer bars'.

AN article in the Spanish newspaper *El Correo Español*, headed '*Glasgow, muerte y resurreccion*', focused on the city's football culture.

Beside a photograph of Hampden strewn with beer and wine bottles (as it was in the old days, they emphasise) the reporter tells of a visit to Ibrox where he found the fans singing '*un himno estremecedor*'. *Estremecedor* means literally shivering or shuddering.

The song, even translated into Spanish, should be familiar:

Hola, hola, somos los muchachos de Billy
Hola, hola, nos conoceras por nuestro ruido

Con sangre de catolicos hasta la rodilla
Rindete o moriras
Somos los muchachos de Billy.

We are sure no translation is necessary and we look forward to hearing it from the terraces if the Gers draw a Spanish club in the European Cup.

BOOZE

The section on alcoholic drink is necessarily short because ardent spirits and heavy ales have played little part in the 12 years of the *Herald Diary*:

THE National Trust for Scotland had the honour of running the most upmarket shebeen in Scotland. The shebeen (which, as you will all no doubt know, is an illegal drinking den) operated at the Trust's headquarters in Edinburgh's douce Charlotte Square.

The Trust's executive committee met there on a monthly basis and,

before lunch, refreshments of an alcoholic nature were served.

The chaps on the executive, not wishing to spend the revenue donated by Trust members, were in the habit of organising a pay bar where the likes of your Marquess of Bute and the Earl of Wemyss and March would fork out for their gin and tonic, dry sherry, or can of Tennents Super.

All very laudable, canny, and cost conscious – but totally illegal since the Trust did not have a licence to sell excisable liquor on their premises.

The illegality of it all did not go unnoticed by a disenchanted former member of staff who blew the gaff to Lothian Police licence division. The police were obliged to turn up at the lunch, interrupt the talk of heritage and history, and advise the Trust that their upper-class drinking den must close forthwith.

KICK like a mule . . . On a trip to Cyprus courtesy of the RAF, the Diary was introduced to a wine called Kokkinelli. It is a kind of Cypriot Lanliq, made of already strong local red wine fortified with brandy. Kokkinelli is consumed in great quantities by British airmen, especially since it is provided

DANGER
Please take alternative path
to cemetery when anglers
are cásting here as there
is a danger of being hooked

free with meals in many of the small
tavernas near the bases.

The wine can have unusual side
effects. One airman, under its influence, hijacked a donkey from the
village to get back to base. When chal-
lenged by the guard at the gate, he
spurred on the donkey and tried to persuade it to jump over the barrier. The
donkey refused but the airman flew
over the barrier beautifully, landing at
the feet of the military policeman.

Another imbiber made it safely back
to his quarters where he proceeded to
hang his clothes over his bed before
falling asleep in the wardrobe.

Kokkinelli is a precocious little
wine, as they say in the Gallowgate.

A PRECOCIOUS nine-year-old enters
a public house and shouts to the waitress to bring him a whisky.

The waitress looks at the height of
him and asks: 'Do you want to get me
into trouble?'

'Maybe later,' he says, 'but get me
that drink first.'

A PLUMBER carrying out a job of
work for a genteel Ayr lady was suffering from the effects of a ferocious
hangover. He persevered with the
work in hand and the lady, spotting
that he was in need of some refreshment, asked: 'Would you like an
apple?'

He considered the kind offer and,
concluding that it did not quite meet
the needs of his predicament, declined.

'Well, then, how about a half?' she
asked.

'Oh, I'm sure I could manage that,'
he responded brightly – at which point
the lady produced a knife and cut the
apple in two.

BURNS

A CANNIBAL chief was guest of honour at a Burns Supper organised by the white administrator in a British outpost of West Africa. The chief thoroughly enjoyed the ritual, the drink, but most of all the food, of which he partook mightily.

At one point the company were asked to be upstanding. 'What are we doing now?' the chief inquired.

'We're going to toast the lassies,' his host told him.

'No thanks, I couldn't eat another thing,' the chief replied.

SPEAKING at Burns Suppers can be a frightening proposition and speakers have been known to take refuge in strong drink. This can be dangerous.

Take the case of one chap, who shall remain nameless, who was to give the Toast to the Lassies. He had consumed so much whisky by the time it came for him to speak that all he could do was stagger to his feet, sway about a bit, blurt out 'Fair fa' your honest, sonsy face, chieftain o' the puddin' race', and collapse in his seat.

THEN there was the speaker who turned up to give the Immortal Memory at a Burns Supper but on the way to the club had suffered an

accident to his dentures. He mumbled his apologies to the club secretary and explained why he would be unable to speak.

The quick-thinking secretary told him not to worry, made a quick phone call and said that help was on its way. Ten minutes later another club member arrived, with a box full of dentures. The speaker was able to find a suitable set and went ahead with his speech.

Afterwards, he approached the secretary and told him that the dentures he found in the box were actually a better fit than his own pair. 'Give my thanks to your dentist friend,' he added.

'I will,' the secretary replied, 'but he isn't a dentist. He's an undertaker.'

BURNS's way with the lassies is recorded in the story of when he was out for a walk in the country. He encountered a beautiful milkmaid in a narrow lane. The milkmaid was carrying two pails on a yoke over her shoulders and there was no room for the two to pass. This gave Burns the chance to indulge in a bit of chat. He asked her if she knew who he was.

'No,' she replied.

'I'm Rabbie Burns,' he told her.

'In that case, I suppose I'd better put these pails down right now,' she said.

AN American tourist visiting Ayrshire at the height of the Burns season was delighted to be invited to a Supper. He said proudly that he already knew quite a bit about the Bard. He could even quote from Burns's poem about Ayr:

Ayr, there's no' a toon surpasses
For pullin' tails off horses' asses.

A REGULAR Burns speaker, who again shall remain nameless, appeared at a Supper where the turnout was quite small. At the end of the evening, the secretary offered him a fee, which he declined as the club was obviously not affluent. The delighted secretary announced this to the members with the information that the money saved would go into a special fund 'to allow us to afford some really good speakers next year'.

A CHAP from Cumbernauld gave us this recollection of the time he was invited to play the piano at a local Celtic supporters' club Burns Night.

'That the evening was not going to be one for the purists became evident when the first singer ("Ah'll jist start and you foallie") opened with the well-known Burns song *Galway Bay*. The *Wild Colonial Boy* was demanded as an encore.'

The sangs and clatter continued, with Kevin Barry giving his young life, Sean South approaching barracks walls, and glorious St Patrick being hailed. The evening deteriorated further when a member of the audience threw a screwtop at the portrait of Rabbie Burns on the wall on the grounds that 'that Masonic bastard's been staring doon at us a' night'.

At the end of the night, the chairman, ignoring the pianist's request for anonymity, said: 'I'd like to thank the pianist, William Waddell.'

The chairman managed to assuage the bears growling at the mention of William Waddell by saying: 'C'mon, he widnae know a' oor songs if he wisnae a Tim.'

HUGH McNamee recalls the occasion he was asked to play the piano at a Burns Night at the social club of a factory in Bridgeton.

'I noticed, after playing the first verse of the well-known songs, a poor response to the other verses. Some poems were spoken rather badly and it began to dawn on me that the gentlemen were not particularly knowledgeable about the Bard but were more intent on a good night out, an impression confirmed by the amount of whisky on the tables.'

When he played some of the lesser-known songs, there was even less response and after a time Mr McNamee was approached by one of the guests, who said: 'Hey, Jimmy. F*** Burns. Let's have *Singing the Blues.*'

COONCILLORS

The world of local government is a rich source of material for Diary columns. Where would we be without our cooncillors?

HANDY HINTS FOR WOULD-BE COUNCILLORS: When attending selection conferences where, as in Strathclyde and Glasgow, the actual election takes place, you may be asked on which committee you would like to

serve, if elected. Do not reply 'The Licensing Board' as did one hopeful for a vacant Govan seat. This answer is open to misinterpretation where graft has not always meant hard work.

The correct answer is, of course, Social Work or Education.

IN March 1980, the cooncillors of Clydebank were faced with the issue of finding a name for the district council's new headquarters. The SNP members advocated Saltire House. The lone Tory came up with Thatcher House. The ruling Labour group, of course, rejected both – in favour of the name Municipal Buildings. An example of the ingenuity which has made Clydebank what it is today.

THE annual appeal to local authorities for grant aid by the Scottish National Orchestra led to some earnest discussion at Cumnock and Doon Valley District Council.

Under guidelines from the Convention of Scottish Local Authorities, the council should have given £1,600 to the national orchestra. They decided to give £250. One councillor said that this was a niggardly amount and proposed

29

have failed to see their number rise above half a dozen out of 60 seats. They have to get their fun somehow.

In May 1985, Councillor Ian Dyer took exception to the fact that the Labour members decided to have the city's parks department provide flowers and shrubbery to decorate a stall at a CND rally at the Kelvin Hall. He realised he could not stop the proposal going ahead. He did move an amendment, however, that the parks department's sole contribution to the decoration of the stall should be a display of rhubarb. He was defeated.

that the SNO should at least receive parity with the Dalmellington Silver Band and be awarded £500. After some discussion, it was decided to stick to the sum of £250. 'If the SNO want more, it's time they started to give performances at the local gala days,' one cooncillor commented.

ONE would-be Labour cooncillor who broke the mould was Mr Richard Mowbray. He contested Glasgow Kelvinside in April 1980. His most erudite election leaflet was headed 'Tory Economic Fallacies: Their consequences and alternatives' and included such footnotes as 'See Commission of the European Communities Review 1979/80 Table 6.1'.

LIFE is tough for Tory cooncillors in Glasgow, who for the last few years

ONE of the sports at Glasgow City Chambers over the years has been spotting the cooncillors and officials with the biggest appetites in the official dining-room. One tribune of the people – seen consuming the soup, melon balls, a mountain of cold meat, a hot dish, and two puddings – rapidly became known as Two Dinners. Another, observed working his way through seven portions of haddock, was christened The Fishermen's Friend.

ONE of the legends of local government in Scotland is Mr Charles Horsburgh, clerk to the Glasgow licensing board. He is famous for putting publicans through the hoops as he enforces the licensing laws to the letter. Take the case of Granny Black's pub, who decided to add their bit to the yuppification of Glasgow's Merchant City *arrondissement* by putting a smart black and gold canopy on its façade.

Yes, says Mr H, but under the Act, the pub must lose its existing afternoon licence and close between 2.30 p.m. and 5 p.m. because the canopy changes the appearance of the premises.

But surely the canopy is outside the building and not part of the licence?, argue the pub's lawyers. No, the canopy is attached and must be licensed, says Mr H. Oh good, say the pub owners, now customers can sit under the canopy and enjoy continental-style pavement service. No, says Mr H, the pavement is not licensed, only the canopy. The customers could drink on the canopy but not under it.

The owners decided not to proceed with the idea of the canopy.

A NUMBER of cooncillors, from Greenock so the story goes, were on a social outing, or a 'bus run' as it is more properly called. On the way home, the treasurer of the outing announced that there had been a miscalculation and there was a deficit of £15. What was to be done? he asked the good men of the cooncil.

One chap had no doubt: 'I move we give the £15 deficit to the driver.'

We think this may be the same cooncillor who made the famous statement at Greenock Corporation: 'Allegations have been made about me. And I know who the alligators are.'

A GLASGOW Corporation cooncillor was on civic duty at the City Chambers. He had two functions to attend. The first was to hand out commemorative badges to bus drivers and conductors who were leaving the Corporation's employ. The second was to greet a dozen television executives from African countries who were on a course at a Glasgow college and were being entertained to a civic dinner in the Satinwood Suite of the Chambers.

As usual, on both these occasions the civic hospitality was lavish and by the time he was wheeled in to meet the African TV people, the cooncillor had partaken too well of the Chambers' wines.

The Africans were bemused and their college hosts stunned to see the cooncillor hand out commemorative bus badges with the words: 'If it hudnae been for people like you, Glasgow's transport system would huv ground to a halt years ago.'

AN Ayrshire bailie was dealing with a man accused of stealing from his employer. The man had no defence but the bailie ruled: 'Since you have been with your firm for 32 years, I find the case not proven.'

The same bailie frequently 'abolished' accused who had been found guilty.

THE scene is Dundee Trades Council, where a discussion is taking place on ways to broaden the appeal of the May Day rally. One member proposes that

31

tured into the world of community councils. But we were prepared to make an exception in the case of the December meeting of Largs Community Council.

The good burghers of the jewel of the Clyde were discussing the manner in which the local district council was spending cash from the Common Good Fund. As the community council minutes put it: 'Councillor Boyd stated that our district councillors were throwing the money about like drunken sailors in Singapore, and when questioned about this analogy she confirmed having knowledge and experience in this area.'

the Vegetarian Society be invited to set up a stall. This is vetoed by the chairman, obviously a carnivore as well as a Stalinist, with the wonderfully Dundonian statement: 'If the vegetarians take over we'll end up as a banana republic.'

IT was not often that the Diary ven-

THE Scottish local government Ombudsman told in an annual report of a letter he had received from a research student.

The would-be academic, who addressed the Ombudsman as 'Councillor', wanted to know his party's view of 'Public Ignorance of Local Authorities'.

DIDN'T WE HAVE A LOVELY TIME THE DAY WE ESCAPED THE ELECTION

Tom Shields, football fan and champion of lost causes like Scots victories at Wembley, was given time off from election coverage for good behaviour. In this touching letter of gratitude he recounts his deterioration as a political animal by the hour.

To the Editor,
Glasgow Herald

Dear sir,

Thank you for the three-day pass away from writing about the General Election. I used the time to visit London with some friends from the Park Bar in Glasgow who were going down to see Scotland playing England at Wembley.

In case Mr Ted Croker, secretary of the English Football Association, should read this, it must be emphasised that these chaps, although called Macleod, MacDonald, Campbell, and McKinnon and speaking Gaelic a lot, are really of English descent and have not obtained their Wembley tickets by deceit.

They were driven north to find work during the Home Counties Clearances of which Mr Croker has no doubt heard.

Anyway these Park Bar chaps have their own bus which they use to travel to events of social and cultural interest. The trips so far have been to Spain for the World Cup and to Switzerland for the European championship game involving Scotland.

The bus is a 29-seater Bedford which first saw the light of day in 1961, the year England beat Scotland 9-3. How's that for an omen.

It has been converted, with bunk beds, toilet and kitchen sink to take 12 passengers to Scotland's football matches in barely discernible discomfort.

The venture is nearly wrecked at the outset when 12 £11 tickets sent recorded delivery by Cousin Murdo from the Croft in Milton Keynes a week ago fail to arrive. (Does Mr

33

Croker have a part-time job as post-man, too?)

Fortunately Wembley tickets in Glasgow on Tuesday night are about as scarce as a flute band in Bridgeton on July 12 and replacements are easily obtained.

The journey begins outside the Park Bar just after 11 p.m. (a strange time to start a journey one might think but presumably the Park Bar bus veterans know best).

It is 3 a.m. and we are having breakfast at Trust House Forte's charming motorway bistro at Charnock Richard. They must have Ted Croker as a consultant.

It is 4.30 a.m. and we are just short of Derby. The bus has had to stop for some work on the defective fuel line. Bonny Prince Charlie had much the same trouble, remarks Callum, one of the Park Bar bus's veterans.

It is 11 a.m. The Park Bar bus is in pole position in the Wembley Stadium car park. Our next-door neighbour is a small grey van of uncertain vintage.

It is driven by a young chap wearing a kilt of even more uncertain vintage and a three-foot-wide tartan sombrero.

He is singing 'Spot the Looney'. In an otherwise deserted car park it is not difficult to do so.

It is 3 p.m. at Trafalgar Square and the Scots fans are having what can best be described as a garden party. It is very busy and some of the chaps have climbed up on to the fountains obviously to get a better view of the proceedings.

There is a great number of Scottish

fans here for the match despite Mr Croker's efforts to keep them away.

A straw poll reveals that 55% of them are here like me to avoid the election, 10% are here on business, 10% are job-hunting, and 25% don't know.

A substantial number just happen to be wearing tartan and have had Wembley tickets thrust upon them, probably by Cousin Murdo from the Croft in Milton Keynes.

There is a handful of arrests of Scots fans. The endlessly diplomatic London bobbies say the arrests are simply to protect the fans and the general public.

Callum suspects they are lifting Scots with tickets intended for English fans and that Mr Croker has a part-time job as a police informer.

It is 5 p.m. on the Tube to Wembley and every carriage, whether they like it or not, has its own Scottish choir.

'No swearing, boys,' says the choir leader in our carriage and then leads off into a repertoire which includes:

'I wish I was a kettle,
I'd be steaming every day.'

It is 6 p.m. and denizens of the Park Bar bus are receiving Cousin Murdo from the Croft in Milton Keynes with numerous other relatives and friends for a pre-match cocktail.

In fact, the whole car park resembles a giant tartan cocktail party. The fellow in the uncertain kilt and the tartan sombrero is back again singing 'Spot the Looney.'

In the crowded car park it is more difficult to do so but not impossible.

It is 7.10 p.m. and the English FA have just announced that tickets can still be bought at the stadium. You don't even have to be English to buy them. Mr Croker's racist attitude to Scots fans obviously has not stopped him from extracting the maximum financial advantage for the English FA from the fixture. The attendance is 84,000 and receipts £654,000.

It is 7.45 p.m. and the game begins. For further details please consult Jim Reynolds, of our sports pages or possibly the obituary column.

It is 10 p.m. and the Park Bar bus piper, I think his name is Callum, is playing a lament in the Wembley car park. Another bus veteran, obviously inured to disappointment has cheered up and is asking a fetching WPC to dance.

It is midnight. The 12 Callums and I have gone out to enjoy a drink and a bit of crack, as the Highlanders put it. We should also celebrate Jock Stein's and Graeme Souness's last game in charge of Scotland, at least according to Callum.

The trouble is London is closed, at least to Scottish fans.

We find ourselves outside a club in Kensington High Street. The bouncer explains that it is a gay club.

'No problem,' says Callum grasping hold of my hand and adding: 'It's terrible what you have to do here to get a late drink in London. I've had more fun in Benbecula on a Monday night.'

It is 3 a.m. We take a taxi back to the bus at Wembley Stadium. The chap in the tartan sombrero has stretched out in a tartan sleeping-bag beside his van. There is only time for a quick chorus of 'Spot the Looney' before retiring to the relative comfort of the bus.

It is 10 a.m. on Friday morning and the bus is heading north. Looking on the bright side we discuss Scotland's chances in the under-21 World Cup in Mexico.

By coincidence one of the Callums has a sister who lives just outside Mexico City who, he is sure, would put us up.

By a narrow margin the vote is to head north and not for Mexico City.

But before this business in Mexico is over I would not count on the Park Bar contingent having a presence in Central America.

Meanwhile, for some, it is back to the election.

ESCAPE TO SIBERIA

Siberia, once the one-way ticket destination for Soviet deportees, is now desperate to attract visitors of a different kind as talk switches from hard labour to hard currency. Tom Shields has been there – and returned to tell this tale.

THE Russians sent me to Siberia. In a break with tradition they let me back out after a fortnight so that I could tell you lot what a splendid holiday spot it is. It is, I can tell you lot, a splendid holiday spot. That is, if you can call a place that is bigger than the US a spot. Anyway, Intourist is hotter than ever in pursuit of tourist hard currency. But Moscow and Leningrad, the traditional Russian visitor venues, are full to bursting.

Siberia, the land of pioneers, prisoners and political exiles, still has plenty of space. Intourist is selling Siberia as the great outdoors adventure, which is why I found myself in the company of experts on hiking, rambling, fishing, bird-watching, cycling, and sundry other healthy activities.

There was also an Irishman whose speciality was finding the local pub, investigating the level of crack in Siberia, and nosing around the shops. This seemed like a more interesting adventure. I decided to follow the Irish itinerary.

So here we are in Abakan which, as I'm sure you know, is capital of the ancient land of Khakassia. Sunny Khakassia, as it is rightfully called, for the annual average is 300 days of sunshine. This land is famous for its fertile soil and rich mineral resources, full-flowing rivers and healthful lakes and for its taiga, abundant in mushrooms, berries and nuts.

37

OK, I admit all that last bit is straight from the Intourist brochure. The reality is that the town looks a bit like Drumchapel. There is nothing in the shops unless you want a pair of plastic sandals. There are no postcards of Abakan but there are views of Leningrad and Samantha Fox's chest.

The souvenir shop in the hotel is empty, but in the lift I am offered a soldier's hat for £5, which seems like a bargain. I decline the offer to buy the medals from the Afghanistan war.

The hotel offers little for those of us on the hedonist adventure trip. It has none of the facilities you would expect in a Western hotel, although it does have a cement mixer in the foyer.

It has a bar which is open only four hours a day in this neo-prohibitionist land. Inspection of the rest of downtown Abakan reveals that the hotel is actually the liveliest spot around. In a leafy square some of the locals are passing round a big glass container of brown liquid. It is apple juice, and this is what the Abakan lads mean by going out for a jar.

When the bar opens later we discover it is selling apple juice, ice cream, and vodka if you ask nicely. At closing time a local is spectacularly sick over the bar counter. Was it too much apple juice or simply a bad ice cream?

Abakan, it has to be said, is not great for the crack, but the other special interests are thriving. The bird watcher has been down at the riverbank and has seen a white-throated needletail, a sparrowhawk and a pippet. Someone else has been horse-riding at a farm run by the Soviet union of miners. The cyclist has teamed up with a local wheelers' club whose membership seems to consist entirely of blonde nymphets in Lycra trousers. He is now enviously referred to as the pedalophile.

Us less active tourists have been taking in Shushenskoye, the village where Lenin spent his years of Siberian exile. Compared with the living conditions of the present-day Abakanites, whom he freed from Tsarist slavery, Lenin spent his Siberian exile in some comfort in a substantial wooden house with a sauna. Shushenskoye looks for all the world like an olde-worlde timeshare development.

There is some great shopping to be done at the Shushenskoye souvenir stall. Badges and busts of Lenin galore. Samantha Fox's bust is also available in key ring or postcard form.

On, farther east, to Irkutsk, the capital of the Buryat region and the oldest city in Siberia. From here the first Russian caravans of merchants set off to China and Mongolia. The look of Irkutsk reflects its 300-year-old history. It boasts many ancient stone buildings of original architecture and time-blackened wooden mansions. (Yes, that's the Intourist brochure speaking again.) In Scottish terms, I would place Irkutsk as a lively but faded Paisley. In Russian terms, it's a shopper's paradise.

Bookshops with marvellous posters costing pennies. Record shops with Paul McCartney and Elton John LPs or the boxed sets of Bolshoi operas for

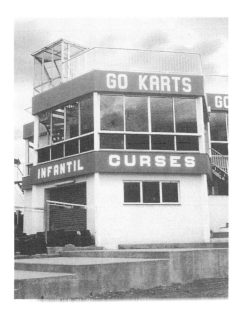

under £2. Brilliant jewellery made from local semi-precious stones.

The local Harrods has a magnificent moose's head on sale for 490 roubles (about £49). I want to buy but can hardly lift it, never mind carry it home. The people in the shop are very sympathetic but no, they do not deliver to Glasgow.

There is a busy market-place where you can have your photo taken with a real live tiger. A small, chained up, real live tiger. But still it looks a risky business.

A kiosk is selling photographs of the Tsar, poor photocopies of a sex manual, and full colour posters of our Samantha.

In winter, when the temperature descends to minus 40 degrees centigrade, the Irkutsk market sells milk in blocks. I pine for the opportunity to

ask people if they would like one lump or two in their tea. But the autumn weather is hot. The trouble with Siberia is that in the winter it is all ice and in the summer there is no ice.

The Irkutsk market has more fresh fruit and veg than I had seen in the rest of Russia put together. The giant watermelons are an essential purchase. The chances are in Siberia if you're on the hedonist adventure holiday, you will have been sitting up half the night drinking vodka with Mongolians, Russians, Ukrainians, Moldavians or, if you're stuck, Americans.

This leaves you in the morning with a thirst. In most places a soft drink is out of the question. So is mineral water, which Siberian hotels appear not to sell until lunchtime.

The tap water is not recommended. Any milk on the breakfast table will be of the soor milk cairt variety. There is usually a jug of juice which will vary in colour from purple to green, yellow to brown, depending on the berries from which it is squeezed. This juice is not the berries and will not quench your morning thirst.

But the watermelon will. It is your Siberian diet Irn Bru.

The hotel is comfortable and caught in a fascinating time-warp. *Yellow Submarine* is playing on the video in the foyer. In the tourist hard-currency bar, a Californian rock band called Alien Blackness, all long hair and cowboy boots, is enjoying its three-month Siberian tour, paid for out of the Soviet Government's arts budget.

But what are the outdoors people up

to? They are at Lake Baikal, the world's largest freshwater lake, which is just up the road. Baikal is a unique creation of nature, striking with its primordial beauty. (Yes, we're back into the Intourist brochure.) Its water is crystal clear and transparent – apart from the bit that's polluted by the pulp mill, but that will be closed by 1992.

Some of the outdoor activists are away fishing. In typical Russian style, it involves more than getting into a boat and dangling a line in the water. They sail away for half a day and spend the night in a hut in a small settlement where the locals make them buckets of borsch for their tea. At 2 a.m. they are wakened and taken out to a raft where they fish by floodlight.

It is a great adventure and it doesn't really matter that they don't catch a single fish. This is surprising since Lake Baikal has 2,500 species of fish. With all these varieties, it is puzzling that every day the hotel serves the same kind of fish. Thankfully it is tasty, a kind of salmon or trout called omul.

The activists have a choice of hiking, climbing, sub-aqua, wind-surfing, and sailing. The less-activists can lie on the sandy beach or sample a Russian steam bath.

The pedalophile wishes it was winter when the lake freezes over and you can cycle on it. The bird-watcher is ecstatic: he has just seen a capercaillie and a Siberian tit.

There is no sign, however, of Samantha in the souvenir shop. But I have found, through the free economy market, a splendid set of antlers for only £30. All I have to do is get them back to Glasgow via Ulan-Ude, Yakutsk, Moscow, Leningrad and London.

Say what you like about Aeroflot. The uncertain in-flight food (well, why not a Penguin biscuit for your dessert?); the certainty that your in-flight refreshment will be a cup of some coloured juice; and the flies buzzing around the cabins (there must be some extremely far-travelled Russian flies).

But Aeroflot's relaxed policy on hand luggage is brilliant. A set of antlers? No problem.

We're off, antlers and all, to Ulan-Ude, the southernmost stop on my Siberian adventure. This capital of the Buryat region, bordering Mongolia, is the original outpost of the Cossacks and today retains much of its remote, frontier atmosphere. (Yes, more brochure-speak.) Architecturally, much of Ulan-Ude is like Castlemilk. Except Castlemilk does not have a Buddhist monastery or a 30-ft high bronze head of Lenin.

Ulan-Ude also has the most strikingly beautiful women in all the Russias. The Irishman says so and in these matters I bow to his considerable expertise.

The Buddhists, I have to say, are a bunch of nippy sweeties. I got a row for having my hands in my pockets inside the temple. And I thought I was conducting an intelligent interview with the chief lama, asking how he spent a typical day. (He prays a lot, talks to his flock, and watches TV at night; favourite programme the *Nine*

O'Clock News.)

All very nice and ethnographic, I thought, until one of the Russians tells me that during the interview the lama asked the interpreter: 'Why is this man asking me so many stupid questions?' To think I could have been away spotting eagles with the birdman.

There was nothing but friendliness, however, at Yakutsk, the last and most northerly stop on the Siberian tour. Yakutsk is near the Arctic Circle, a town built on concrete pillars in the permafrost zone.

In Scottish terms, it is Stornoway on ice. A wild, isolated place which for eight months of the year is cut off from the rest of the world.

Because of its isolation, the hotel facilities are of a basic nature. An English member of our party decides that his bathroom constitutes too much of an adventure, even for Siberia. 'You can't ask me to sit on this!' he shouts, brandishing a rather pitted and scratched toilet seat at the receptionist. Then he throws the toilet seat across the foyer and storms back to his room.

The Irishman is able to put the matter into perspective. 'Would you have that sanded down and delivered to my room? I don't have a toilet seat at all.'

Yakutsk is the least promising of the Siberian venues but it provides the best food I tasted in two weeks in Russia. The occasion was a boat trip on the River Lena to a picnic site. In Siberian fashion, the round trip by hydrofoil is 300 miles. The landscape is straight out of a Yukon adventure movie.

There is a sign which says do not drop litter and do not chase the bears. I promise not to do either.

While the activists scale the Lena Pillars, the hedonists sit at the camp fire and watch Alosha, the 17-year-old YTS chef, and his wee sister Lana who has skived school to help him, make a magnificent fish soup and some wonderful Siberian stovies. There is champagne and brandy to wash it down. You could get to like the great outdoors.

The Irishman, who is allergic to the great outdoors, has been exploring Yakutsk and has found a Moldavian rock band on tour. He learns that Yakutsk can be a wild place at night with the odd drug addict and mugger lying in wait for miners who come into town with their pockets stuffed with roubles.

41

One of the Moldavians says that if you are going out late, do what he does and carry a big stick.

After a noisy and hectic gold-rush style night in the hotel dining-room (complete with Wild West fight) I decide to retire early to wrap up my antlers.

The Irishman does not want to waste the last night in Siberia. He ventures into the night' clutching a bottle of vodka and a big stick to go to a party he's heard about.

It's an adventurous life in Siberia.

EDUCATION

The Diary's occasional forays into the world of education are invariably due to concerned individuals writing to give us an insight into school life. To be more exact, teachers tell of the idiocies of their pupils, parents tell us of the teacher's latest fit of madness, and everybody gets in touch to tell the world about the headmaster's latest manifestation of believing he is God.

A LETTER arrived at a Strathclyde school, addressed to a Mrs Youing. The staff worked out that it was intended for their Mrs Ewing. The letter was from a former pupil of the school. Mrs Ewing wondered why he had written to her since she had never actually

had the pleasure of teaching him. The letter made it all clear: 'I am writing to you because your name is the only one I can spell.'

STRATHCLYDE Regional Council's further education subcommittee know how to be brief and to the point. Consider this minute from one of their meetings: 'With reference to the minutes of the Community Development Committee when that committee had considered a report commissioned by the Glasgow Divisional Deprivation Group relative to Community Development in Springburn and had agreed to continue consideration of the matter to allow the chairman and the vice-chairman of that committee to discuss the report with appropriate members and officials in the first instance, the subcommittee, having considered the said report, agreed to continue consideration of the matter pending the outcome of the discussion referred to.' Got that?

A CIRCULAR on the role of head teachers in primary schools, issued by the Committee on Primary Education, contained this piece of double-think:

'In accordance with precedent, the head teacher is referred to as he and the class teachers as she. No discrimination is intended.'

THE department of artificial intelligence at Edinburgh University was working on computer programmes which would be able to translate speech instantaneously from one language to another. A difficult task, as you can imagine. One test proved just how difficult. When the phrase 'the spirit is willing but the flesh is weak' was translated into Russian and back into English, it came out as 'the vodka is strong but the meat is rotten'.

A MATHS teacher in a school on the south side of Glasgow decided to make the arithmetic exam more interesting for some of the under-achievers in his class. He framed questions to which the class could relate. They had to estimate, for instance, the extra profit earned by a shopkeeper who sold cigarettes and matches singly compared to selling by the packet. Another question asked the pupils to work out a complex betting slip.

The class were unusually absorbed in their exam. The silence was only broken when one boy put up his hand to ask why the punter had not paid his tax on the betting slip.

GLASGOW students have their own rhyming slang name for a lower second honours degree, or two-two as it is known in academic circles. It is called a Desmond, after the well-known South African bishop.

THE owner of a Renfrewshire printing firm was interviewing candidates for an apprenticeship. The businessman was very hot on literacy and numeracy, attributes which he had found very useful in employees. He asked one young man how good his arithmetic was.

'No' bad,' was the reply.

He was then asked to divide 1,000 by four. After a long pause the candidate said: 'Actually, I'm more of a calculator man myself.'

INNUMERACY struck in Greenock, too, where a Diary reader asked an assistant in a bakery shop for a dozen rolls.

'What's a dozen?' he heard the young girl ask an older colleague.

The girl duly put the 12 rolls in a bag. 'Could you make that a dozen and a half, please?' the customer asked.

At which point the assistant cut a roll in half and dropped it into the bag.

AN edict in Strathclyde schools forbade smoking, even by teachers, except in designated rooms. Thus the staff rooms at Eastbank Academy became no-go areas for dominies addicted to the weed. These poor, lost souls had to find alternative accommodation for the burning of the weed and inhalation of nicotine.

Appropriately enough, they took refuge in a disused girls' toilet.

STRATHCLYDE education officials are rigorous in rooting out racist attitudes in their schools. This instance involved a routine visit to a school dining-hall.

One of the dinner ladies was explaining the breakdown of lunching habits among pupils: 'We have the homies, the dinnies, and the packies,' she explained.

After a sharp intake of breath from the visiting high heid yins, the lady was informed that the last word mentioned was not acceptable language.

Luckily she was able to explain that it was not a reference to the children's ethnic origins, merely to the fact that they brought packed lunches to school.

THESE were among the answers given by pupils in a general knowledge quiz held in a school in darkest Lanarkshire. The school will remain unnamed to protect the innocent. (We are talking about the teachers, of course.)

Asked to name the five continents, a darling child replied: 'A, E, I, O, U.' Another ventured that the author of *Treasure Island* was Anneka Rice.

The prize for lateral thinking went to the child who was asked how a blind person would know if he or she had arrived at a pedestrian crossing. The answer, of course, is that there are bumps at edge of the pavement. Nothing so prosaic for this lad, who said the blind person would know 'when the dug stoaps'.

MORE school quiz gems, this time from the rehearsals for the Glasgow Libraries' Primary School Quiz:

- What is the Kremlin? 'A wee furry hing fae that Steven Spielberg fillum.'
- Where are the Crown Jewels kept? 'Oan the Queen's heid.'
- What did Noah send out of the Ark first to see if the flood had stopped? 'His wife.'

PAISLEY polis were involved in a project with local schools, the aim being to teach children how to react to a variety of dangerous situations. One of the exhibits was an ordinary room full of potential nasties such as an iron lying face down on an ironing board and a chip pan brimful of fat.

'Now why mustn't we touch any of these things?' a polisman inquired of a primary seven class from a local school.

'Because we'll leave our finger prints on them,' was the response from one cherubic wee lassie.

FOOD

The *Herald* Taste Day pages are normally devoted to the opinions and prejudices of the consumer. For a change it was the turn of the consumed to have their say.

I have talked to head waiters and chefs from some of our better restaurants about the occasions when the customer was not right. To protect the innocent and the livelihoods of certain head waiters, my informants must remain anonymous.

THERE is an old and oft-repeated joke about a young man in a Glasgow restaurant who is asked by the waiter if he would like ginger with his melon. He replies that he will stick to the red wine, the same as the rest of the company. There is no recorded instance of this happening but the spirit of the untutored diner lives on with the person who ordered steak tartare and then complained that it was raw. Or the customer who asked for his steak tartare well done.

Not to mention the lady who complained to the manager of an Italian restaurant about their practice of providing powdered milk which had made her coffee taste disgusting. Not surprising, he replied, since she had just put two spoonfuls of parmesan cheese into her cup.

Or the customer in a wine bar who ordered soup followed by a main course with a side salad. The waitress placed his cutlery and a bowl containing French dressing on his table and went to the kitchen to fetch his soup. She returned to find the customer eating the bowl of French dressing. She left him to finish this rather unusual soup course and was not surprised when he took refuge in the toilet and was unable to tackle the rest of his meal. Compared to this, the quite common practice of drinking the water from fingerbowls pales into insignificance.

47

There was another obvious connoisseur who told a waiter that there was a leaf floating in the French dressing. It must have blown in through the open door, she added. *Unbayleafable*, the waiter might have said, if he were into elaborate puns.

MOST head waiters will tell you that they do not mind dealing with diners who, faced with a menu bulging with gastronomic goodies, admit that they just want something simple. A well-known Glasgow lawyer is famous for by-passing the glories of haute, nouvelle, and sundry other cuisines in favour of a regular lunchtime order of plain omelette and mashed potatoes, albeit washed down by a bottle of fine wine costing about £20.

Another customer on whom the niceties of à la carte, table d'hôte and surprise menus are obviously lost, plumped for smoked salmon from the list of starters. Asked what else he would like he ordered and received on a side plate a portion of chips and peas.

IT is the customer who thinks he or she knows all about good food and fine wines that causes the most heartache to the chef and head waiter. The owner of an establishment which prides itself on value for money quality wines still remembers with sorrow the Chambertin 1959 which he was offering at the apparently knock-down price of £19.95 a bottle. A customer consulting his wine diary discovered that it was an excep-

tional year. He ordered a bottle only to return it without drinking on the grounds that the wine was a brown colour and not red. Instead of trying to explain about the changes in colour as a wine ages, the chef took the bottle back and shared it with a wine-loving customer who was also in the restaurant. The wine waiter, unable to resist a comment to the offending diner, asked him if he had managed to retain the nice pink colour he had been born with.

The same chef has had his wild strawberries, brought in triumph from the market, rejected by a diner, who said they were too small.

THERE is a school of thought among head waiters that there is a growing band of professional complainers: people who are convinced they can get a free meal, a reduced bill, or even a free drink just by being difficult.

One person complained that the pheasant was of a poor standard. He took his complaint as far as the consumer problem page of a Sunday newspaper before admitting that it was in fact the first time he had ever tried pheasant and had no idea how it should taste.

Another difficult customer demanded a 50 per cent reduction on his bill. The food had been excellent, he said, but the waiter should have informed him of the various other menus he could have had. Where other diners produce a credit card to pay he placed his lawyer's card on the table. The waiter stood firm, phoned the police, received full payment and is still awaiting the writ.

THE problem of menu items not being available for the customer has been around for a long time. There was a famous waitress employed at a West Coast hotel during the 1950s, hey-day of bus and steamer trips from Glasgow. One day, by chance a Friday, due to a typist's error haddock and chips was missing from the lunch menu. The waitress, whose speed and dexterity could have won any Trencherman award for service, but who unfortunately sounded like Francie or Josie's first cousin, was told to inform the customers of the omission, as briefly as possible.

This she did, by standing at the door of the restaurant and calling out, 'Hauns up a' youse yins that are Cathlics.'

OTHER forms of skulduggery which are by no means uncommon in restaurants include leaving by mistake with the wrong coat or umbrella. The Marks and Spencer raincoat swapped for the Burberry is a good trick.

One restaurant in Glasgow is still trying to remedy the situation where a regular and valued customer is using a new umbrella he inadvertently picked up instead of his own battered specimen some months ago.

THERE is antisocial behaviour which is not deliberate but which is usually alcohol-induced. A waiter who worked in the old 101 Restaurant in Glasgow recalls an upmarket but rather well-oiled lady diner who plunged down a flight of steps. Only slightly hurt but in a state of considerable shock she was asked by a member of staff who was comforting her as she lay on the floor if she would like a medicinal brandy. 'Make it a whisky and soda,' was the reply.

Also from the 101 days comes the

story of a beautifully turned-out woman who had also enjoyed too much wine. She went to the ladies and walked back through the restaurant with the back of her skirt tucked inside her knickers. It fell to the poor head waiter to inform her of the situation.

But when it comes to bad behaviour in restaurants the Americans lead the field . . .

A Texan complete with boots and stetson was not prepared to wait his turn in the cocktail bar along with other customers who had not booked a table in a busy hotel restaurant. When a table became vacant he jumped the queue and sat down. The waiters, in a scene reminiscent of a *Scotch and Wry* sketch, ignored his constant shouts to be given a menu. Eventually the head waiter simply walked up and took away the table leaving the Texan sitting in a chair in the middle of the restaurant. He got the message and returned to the bar.

Another American customer resident in one of Scotland's better hotels was getting firmly on the waiters' nerves with his regular demand, 'Hey boy, get me a pitcher of water.' One morning he made this request in his usual loud voice to a waiter who was not feeling at his best. The waiter walked over to an oil painting of a river scene which adorned the restaurant wall. He took it down and handed it to the American with the words: 'Here is your picture of water, sir.' The American didn't get the joke. The waiter was suspended for a week.

FOOTBALL

The game of football featured as prominently in the Diary as it does in the Scottish male psyche. The stories were mainly unclassifiable and those repeated below are in no particular order:

WHEN Jock Wallace was manager of Leicester City FC, his strong accent and use of Scottish patois left some of his English players on the bewildered side. After one team briefing, a number of them surrounded Scots player Eddie Kelly to ask the question: 'What's a scoosh case?'

SCOTLAND skipper Roy Aitken left the Cypriot press somewhat confused before a 1989 World Cup qualifier by telling them that Scotland 'were going to get wired in . . . '

SOCCER in the USA is a whole different ballgame. We have become used to cheerleaders, Wurlitzers, and five action replays of each goal. But will we ever accept the term used by Tampa Bay Rowdies to describe their supporters? Down Tampa way the bears on the terracing are called fannies.

INSIGHT into the essentially warm-hearted nature of the Old Firm rivalry.

On the retirement of Willie Waddell, after a successful career as a player, manager and director of Rangers, Jock Wallace, Rangers' manager, said: 'I have no comment to make.'

Desmond White, chairman of Celtic, said: 'This is Rangers' business and has nothing to do with Celtic, so I have no comment to make . . . '

JAMIE Fairley, a talented midfielder on the books of Hamilton Accies in 1980, was expected soon to move on to bigger things. His answers to an interview in the club programme gave an inkling of where his heart lay:

Favourite colour? Green.

Favourite team as a boy? Celtic.

Highlight of career so far? Playing against Celtic in a friendly match.

Person you would most like to meet? His Holiness Pope John Paul II.

Footnote: Jamie Fairley was subsequently transferred, not to Celtic, but to Motherwell FC.

OTHER allegiances were to be discovered in the programme produced by Stenhousemuir FC for their 1986 Skol Cup match against Rangers. It contained profiles of two Stenhousemuir players, Harry Erwin and Jim Sinnet, in which both fairly nailed their colours (blue) to the mast.

Asked to choose their favourite other teams, both named Rangers. Favourite away ground of both was Ibrox. Both named the best goal they had ever seen as one by Davie Cooper for Rangers against Celtic. Favourite players, past and present, were John Greig, Derek Johnstone, and Davie Cooper, with

Maradonna the only non-Ranger to get a mention.

Fair enough, you might think, until you reach the next question: 'Who would you like to throw a bucket of water at?' Mr Erwin replied: 'The Celtic team.' Mr Sinnet said: 'Celtic and T. Burns.'

Mr Sinnet's other entries included: 'Hobbies – going to watch Rangers. Favourite reading material – *Rangers News*.' He also informed us that his favourite listening was 'flute band music'. Mr Erwin won the bad taste award for his entry: 'Favourite funny man – The Pope.'

Footnote: Stenhousemuir later apologised to Celtic.

GEORGE Best graced the Scottish football scene briefly in 1980 with Hibernian FC. Despite his drinking problems, Georgie really did his best for the Hi-Bees. On his departure this was duly acknowledged by the Hibernian Supporters Association. A warm little tale, spoiled only slightly by the association's choice of a whisky decanter and glasses as his going-away present.

THE construction of the new Ibrox Stadium was one of the wonders of the eighties. Two Rangers fans were looking at the stand which had just been completed at the traditional Celtic end of the ground. 'Look at that. Is it no' brilliant?' one opined.

'Aye,' his pal replied. Then after a

pause he added: 'Too good fur thae animals.'

THE administrators of the game of football in Scotland often exhibit quite telling foibles. Thus it was in October 1981 that the Diary reported on a regular practice by Mr David Letham, president of the Scottish Football League and a director of Queen's Park. At a time when football attendances were in decline and Queen's Park faced an uncertain future at Hampden Park, Mr Letham devoted much time and effort to standing guard on Queen's home match days at the first-floor toilets.

This was to ensure that no ordinary QP punters availed themselves of the facilities, despite the fact that the supporters' club bar was adjacent.

This toilet was only for VIPs. The common herd were banished to relieve themselves in the spartan facilities in the turrets.

It was no surprise that Mr Letham was quickly awarded the sobriquet Mr Loo.

BOHEMIANS football club of Dublin were in Glasgow to play Rangers in European competition. At a press conference, a reporter, referring to the possibility of sectarian rivalry spoiling the match, asked the manager of the Dublin team: 'Do you have any reservations about coming to Glasgow to play Rangers?'

'Sure,' he replied, 'we're staying at the Albany.'

ONE of the industries associated with the game of football is that conducted by the urchins who frequent the environs of football stadia and greet arriving motorists with the 'offer' to 'look after your motor, mister'. One visitor to Celtic Park declined the offer and pointed to the Alsatian in the back seat which, he was sure, was security enough. He returned to find all four tyres flat and a note on the windscreen saying: 'Get your Alsatian to blow them up for you.'

THE gentle wit of the Scottish football fan was apparent yet again at the World Cup in Mexico. After the Scots lost 1-0 to Denmark, both sets of fans were hurling friendly chants at each other. Thanks to barriers of accent, if not language, the Danes kept smiling through a little ditty from the Scottish fans which went: *'You can stick your streaky bacon up your arse.'*

LEGEND has it that a bunch of Celtic fans in Bellshill, Lanarkshire, renamed their supporters the John F. Kennedy, in memory of the assassinated American president. Legend also has it that their Rangers counterparts changed their name to the Lee Harvey Oswald Loyal.

THE Rangers fans were quick to

welcome Israeli internationalist Avi Cohen. He came on to the Ibrox turf to the strains of that old song: '*Shalom, shalom, we are the Billy Boys . . .* '

DESPITE having three players with the first name Kevin (McMinn, Drinkell, and MacDonald) Rangers fans never quite got used to this name, with its Romano-Irish overtones. Thus one fan was heard to exclaim: 'Well done, Billy Drinkell.'

FORMER Rangers manager Graeme Souness's unfortunate experiences of being sent off halfway through football matches led to a cocktail being named after him. You simply ask the barman for a Souness.
  'What's a Souness?' he will say.
  'Just one half then I'm off,' is the reply.

WHEN the buying and rapid reselling of players by former Rangers manager Graeme Souness reached its peak in 1988, the club announced that in future team members would have sell-by dates instead of numbers on their jerseys.

THREE international footballers, one Irish, one English and one Scottish, have the same names as birds. Name them. Answer: Bertie Peacock, Frank Swift, and Matt Busby.

IN the autumn of 1988, a run of poor performances by Celtic FC led to a large mailbag which subsequently became known as the Parkhead Jokelist:

Have you seen the new Celtic strip? It has green and white hoops with a red neck.

What's the connection between Celtic's season and the Glasgow Garden Festival? They were both finished by September.

Two men on a desert island. One says: 'That's Celtic beaten again.' 'How do you know?' asks his pal. 'Well, it's Saturday, isn't it?'

Celtic's new signing is Chinese. He is called Win Wan Soon.

The club's new sponsor is Tampax, to help them through this difficult period.

Manager Billy McNeill dug up the pitch at Parkhead in mid-season and planted potatoes. Why? So Celtic would have something to lift at the end of the season.

Goalkeeper Ian Andrews had a short and unfortunate career at Celtic.

What's the difference between Ian Andrews and Eamonn Andrews? they asked. Eamonn was good on the box.

What's the difference between Ian Andrews and Cinderella? Cinderella got to the ball.

What do Ian Andrews and Michael Jackson have in common? They both wear gloves for no apparent reason.

Why is Ian Andrews known as Ena Sharples? Becuase he spends so much time with his head in a net.

There was a disaster at the diamond mine where the Seven Dwarves worked. The wee men were all missing, feared dead. After many hours digging through to the shaft where the dwarves were trapped, the rescuers heard a voice singing: '*Sure, it's a grand old team to play for . . .* '
'At least Dopey's safe,' they were able to report to a worried Snow White.

How did Ken Dodd solve his income tax problems? He sold off his Diddymen to Celtic.

What's the difference between Celtic and the Star of David? The Star of David has six points.

Celtic have signed Steve Davis because they are so many points behind in the premier League they require snookers.

HEART of Midlothian FC have also been the subject of ribald humour. It was rumoured in October 1988 that their goalkeeper Henry Smith was to quit football to work as a salesman in Wallace Mercer's property company. Did he have any experience in this line? Yes, he had recently sold two semis.
Researchers in Edinburgh made a significant breakthrough in AIDS prevention. Wear a pair of Henry Smith's gloves. They never catch anything.

CELTIC hired Lester Piggott as club public relations officer because he was so good at avoiding taxing questions.

ALBION Rovers had a half-back line in the 1970s called Currie, Sage, and Rice.

PELE, who visited Scotland in the summer of 1989 for the junior World Cup, is held in awe by Scottish football fans. Thus when the Great Man, waiting in a crowded departure lounge at Glasgow Airport, got up to give a woman his seat, her husband intervened. 'Don't you know who he is? Give Pele back his seat.'

FATHER Neil McGarrity was one of the young priests ordained by Archbishop Winning in Glasgow in summer 1989. As is usual, he received a gift from friends and parishioners at St Stephen's, Dalmuir. In his case the gift was somewhat unusual: a complete Rangers strip, McEwan's lager logo and all, with the name 'Father Neil' emblazoned on the back.

THE reactions to the separate, but quite similar, problems facing Salman Rushdie and Mo Johnston were the subject of much comment by Diary readers. For example:

Question: What is 6ft 1in, blonde, blue-eyed and lives in Reykjavik?

Answer: Salman Rushdie.

Then there was the tale of the Glasgow taxi driver who was called to pick up a hire at a mosque on the South Side of Glasgow. He had waited for 10 minutes and still had no passenger. He asked for a message to be passed on, but after a further 10 minutes still had not picked up. Exasperated, he finally entered the foyer of the mosque and shouted: 'Taxi for Rushdie!'

Within half an hour of the news that Mo Johnston had signed for Rangers, a Diary reader was on to say that he knew where Mo would be living when he came to Scotland from Nantes in France: 'He's sharing a flat with Salman Rushdie.'

Another fan was on to say: 'At least Salman Rushdie only has the Moslems after him.'

Immediately after the signing, a number of traditional Old Firm songs were being rewritten, such as:

The Soldier's Sash
The Cry Was Mo Surrender
Hello, Hello, We Were the Billy Boys

Rangers fans were to be heard singing:

Hello, hello, Mo is a Billy boy!
Hello, hello, we're glad it's not Big Roy!

We had news of a Rangers fan whose wife had given birth to quadruplets. He decided to call them Eeny, Meeny, Miney and Billy.

It was said that one of the first things Mo Johnston did after spurning Celtic in favour of Rangers was to go to confession. He told the priest: 'Bless me, father, for I have signed . . . '

Celtic fans were claiming that Mo would be sending his children to Judas Iscariot primary school.

A DIARY football peace-keeping award went to Ally McCoist of Rangers.

A player from an opposing team had just been grounded by a robust tackle from Terry Hurlock. 'I'll get you, you English bastard,' the recumbent player shouted.

'Take it easy,' said McCoist as he helped him to his feet. 'Anyway, which one did you mean? There are seven English bastards in the team.'

SCOTTISH goalkeeper Jim Leighton was quoted in *Match Weekly* magazine as saying: 'One of the worst crimes of which a goalkeeper can be found guilty is being caught flat-footed by a long-range, surprise shot that hits the back of the net.'

The next week the luckless goalie suffered the indignity at Hampden Park of seeing a long-range, surprise shot from Norway's Johnsen hit the back of the Scottish net.

THE 1990-91 season was not one of St Mirren's best. They ended bottom of the Premier League. The Diary's man at Love Street had a theory that the choice of pre-match music may have had something to do with it.

'It was bad enough at one home match when the sparsely-populated terraces 30 minutes before kick-off echoed to the sound of the Beatles singing *Look at all the lonely people* ... Worse still was the choice of the last record before the match started – Ray Charles's soulful rendering of *It's Crying Time Again.*

WITH a World Cup match against Norway in the offing, the Diary was sent a useful little publication called *What You Want to Say and How to Say it in Norwegian.*

First we had the familiar chant *Folg, folg* (Follow, follow).

After queuing for a half-time pie, the Norwegian fan would no doubt say: *Mange tak for deres gjaestfrihed* (Many thanks for your hospitality).

In the likely absence of any taxis being available outside Hampden, a more traditional Norwegian form of transport might have come in handy: *Vi onsker at leie et rensdyr* (We wish to hire a reindeer).

Scottish fans wishing to make the Norwegians feel welcome should say: *Kan jeg byde dem noget?* (Can I offer you some refreshments?) On shaking hands with our Norwegian friends, we say: *Set het der* (Put it there).

The phrase-book section, titled 'About Town', had such handy phrases as: *Er der nogen god variete her?* (Is there

a good music hall?) Even handier is: *Hvis vi faar en morsom aften, vii vi betale dem got* (If you give us a good time we will pay you well), not to mention: *Vis os alt* (Show us everything).

There are a few phrases for which, we feared, we would not find a use: *Krol mmine mustacher* (Put the irons on my moustache); *Jeg onsker en friktion* (Put some tonic on my head); and *Server mine eg i et eggeglas* (Serve my eggs in a glass).

It had one phrase which, we hoped, the Norwegians would use after the match: *Jeg er syg* (I am sick).

AFTER one of their fallow seasons there was a report that Celtic were to hold a summer fête at Parkhead. This would have two functions: one, to raise cash; two, it would give them a chance to release some balloons.

It was also said that the Celtic board had definitely decided on the site for a new Parkhead stadium. They also decided not to tell the team the location.

As a precautionary measure, the Parkhead board decided that season tickets for the next year would be in the shape of boomerangs.

THERE was a quick reaction to the news of the appointment of Celtic's new chief executive: 'Terry Cassidy's going to raise £30 million for Celtic? Even Butch Cassidy couldn't raise £30 million for Celtic.'

THE Diary received a (false) news story that Celtic were about to transfer Paul McStay to Blackpool FC. A Parkhead spokesman said no cash was involved in the deal but the 45,000 deckchairs would solve the seating problem at Celtic Park.

THE Gulf War and football came together with this conundrum:

What is the difference between Saddam Hussein and Graeme Souness?

One is a fanatical fundamentalist tyrant who is prepared to sacrifice his people to achieve his aims. The other is president of Iraq.

AN intriguing concept arose out of the bid by the Scottish Professional Footballers' Association to negotiate a share of broadcast fees earned by TV companies.

Ruling on the matter, Trade and Industry Minister Lord Hesketh said that footballers do not enjoy any protection of their 'intellectual property' in the form of playing skills, under the Copyright, Designs, and Patents Act 1988.

The very idea of your average footballer having intellectual anything, never mind intellectual property appealed to the Diary.

Until you start to think about:

- Wee Jimmy Johnstone's jink;
- Jim Baxter's keepie-uppie skill;
- Denis Law's levitation and heading ability;
- Johnny Hubbard's penalty kicks;
- Peter Lorimer's thunderbolt free kicks; and
- Franz Beckenbauer's leadership qualities.

There were some less serious intellectual properties on which certain footballers could claim copyright:

- Gazza's greetin';
- Willie Johnston's Speed;
- Willie Miller's refereeing ability;
- Bobby Moore's light touch;
- Mo Johnston's crossing ability;
- Charlie Tully's cheek;
- Davie Wilson's diving ability;
- Frank Haffey's singing voice;
- Maradonna's handling of the game;
- Derek Johnstone's gravitas;
- Terry Butcher's open door policy;

- Roy Aitken's perserverance (in the face of overwhelming public opinion);
- Tony Higgins's brainpower (unfortunately, all of it in his head);
- Davie Cooper's sinistrality;
- Andy Ritchie's fan dancing;
- George Best's stamina (not solely related to the football pitch);
- Jim McLean's bonhomie;
- Bill Bremner's *sangfroid*;
- Emlyn Hughes's reticence;
- Lou Macari's mental arithmetic (handy in the bookie's);
- Stewart Kennedy's anglophilia;
- Jimmy Greaves's liquidity;
- Bobby Charlton's hair-raising shooting ability;
- Alex Miller's *joie de vivre*.

SOCIAL work departments across the land were ordered by the Government during the Gulf War to set up bereavement counselling teams in readiness for bad news and casualties.

A Strathclyde social worker, asked to fill in a form giving details of his expertise on disaster and trauma counselling, simply entered: 'Celtic supporter.'

OTHER SPORTS

Sports apart from football occasionally fought their way into the columns of the Diary:

RUGBY fans can have an engaging way of negotiating with ticket touts. A conversation outside Murrayfield:

Tout: 'It's £4 for a £1.50 ticket.'
Fan: 'I'll give you £1.50 or I could break your arm and take it from you for nothing.'
Tout: 'It's a deal.'

MANY years of visiting Paris for international matches has given Scottish rugby fans a fair smattering of the French language. One of the leading exponents of this is Mr David Shaw, of Clarkston Rugby Club. The man is damn near bilingual. '*Au secours, mon Robert,*' he can be heard to say in a bar where the prices are rather steep. In a moment of exasperation, he might even be heard to utter: '*Donnez-moi une fracture.*'

Mr Shaw is also credited with making this joke during a weekend in Paris:

Frappez, frappez.
Qui est là?
Nous.
Nous qui?
Certainement!

SOME members at Shotts Golf Club were becoming concerned at the foul language to be heard on the course. A

61

motion banning swearing was put forward at the club AGM. A vote was taken and the anti-swearing lobby was defeated. The golfers of Shotts could continue to rend the air blue – and damn right too.

FANS at an Irish Gaelic football match proved themselves to be no animal lovers. The game, the Offaly senior championship, was delayed when a cockerel sporting the Tullamore colours was thrown on to the pitch. The situation was further confused when a dog started to chase the cockerel around the field. The bird, minus many feathers, avoided the jaws of death by escaping behind an advertising hoarding. The *Irish Times* reported the incident under the memorable heading: 'Dog bites cock at Offaly final.'

PRACTICAL jokes are a way of life in Portree on the Isle of Skye. As evidence, take this story about the Skye Camanachd shinty team. The players in this auspicious outfit, one of the top caman-wielding teams in the country, like to repair to the Tongadale Hotel in Portree of a Saturday night after the match.

After a hard day at the shinty and a few drinks afterwards, the strapping lads of Skye Camanachd have taken, of late, to raiding the fridge in the Tongadale Hotel kitchens which are all too handy for the bar.

Despite warnings from the chef, the shintyists failed to desist from this practice.

The chef, deciding that enough was more than sufficient, baked a pie. It had beautiful, flaky pastry but an unusual filling – Pedigree Chum.

The pie was left in the larder. Sure enough, after closing time, one of the shinty players, who shall remain nameless (although he uses his hands more than other team members), went through to the kitchen, spied the pie, and scoffed the lot.

The midnight snackster was spotted by hotel staff, who knew the provenance of the pie, but, with difficulty, said nothing.

By the time of the next shinty match, the word had gone round the home fans about what had happened. The first the player realised that something was amiss was when there were outbreaks of uncharacteristic barking from the crowd. This was accompanied by the sight of people lifting their legs against the goalposts.

At the hotel, the post-match beer was served in saucers.

It is said that eight of 10 Skye players prefer Pedigree Chum.

FIONA Mackay of Old Kilpatrick told of a visit she made to Old Ranfurly Golf Club in Bridge of Weir, accompanied by a male member of the club.

The problem arose in the bar: 'Drink in hand, I surveyed the room and decided that the best place to sit was near the window, where the players could be seen. As I walked towards a vacant table, my companion was asked by the barmaid to call me back to the bar.

'There, I was informed in embarrassed tones that ladies were not allowed to step off the carpet. The wooden floor was apparently the men's games area. No dividing screens were evident. I enquired from the embarrassed barmaid whether this rule was to stop high heels damaging the hard floor. "No," she replied, "ladies are just not allowed to step off the carpet area."'

BLAIRGOWRIE Golf Club, meanwhile, continue to maintain standards when it comes to dress. In fact, the club has a foolscap sheet of rules and regulations, including such instructions as: gentlemen may wear shorts but only if they are 'tailored' and only if worn with knee-length stockings; and ladies are 'to refrain from wearing brief shorts and suntops in hot weather'.

The Diary's correspondent on the Blairgowrie front does not explain whether the ladies have to go naked in hot weather or whether they can wear brief shorts only in cool weather.

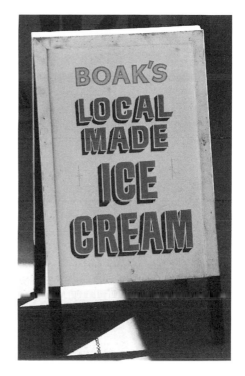

They disqualified him after he admitted starting the race half an hour carly and then cutting numerous corners. His excuse, that he was in a rush to catch the ferry at Stranraer, did not impress the stewards.

THIS story about marathon malpractice just happened to involve an Irishman.

The occasion was the Inverclyde Marathon. A competitor from Antrim in Northern Ireland, who had finished well up the field in a very respectable time, had his medal taken back after an investigation by the race stewards.

THE Welsh are a unique breed, especially when they are at the rugby. The following brief translation guide was produced to help Diary readers understand the Welsh psyche for a visit to Murrayfield:

I was there: Don't tell the wife but I travelled all the way from Cardiff to watch the match in a hotel in Tighnabruaich.

I really was there: I left Cardiff on Tuesday and have since been in every pub in Glasgow and Edinburgh but still don't have a ticket. I am in Ryrie's bar at Haymarket and would pay the £50 asked by the tout for the £10 stand ticket but I have only £3 left from the £500 I had on Tuesday.

This was hardly a classic game of rugby: Scotland really stuffed Wales.

I am still proud of Welsh rugby: I am walking down Rose Street after the match. I am dressed as a dragon and carrying a 10ft leek. I feel really stupid.

I love coming to Scotland. The people are so friendly and we have so much in common what with the mining communities, steel industry, and both our country's aspirations for a greater degree of political independence: Scotland really stuffed Wales and I don't want to talk about the match.

I'll be there in 1993: Yes, we're all coming back to watch the game at the same hotel in Tighnabruaich.

I really will be there in 1993: Yes, I will find my way to Ryrie's bar in Haymarket via pubs in Carlisle, Glasgow, and Bathgate. I will be the one asking people 'Have you got a ticket?' with 10 minutes to go before the kick-off.

FUNERAL FUN

Death has no sting for the *Herald* Diary. Many was the time we turned to the subject of funerals for the odd cheery wee story.

WE were told about the chap whose task it was to arrange the transport at a family funeral. He contacted Strathclyde Buses to provide a coach to take mourners from the church to the crematorium.

Strathclyde Buses carried out the contract with the utmost professionalism. The only, tiny, criticism was that some of the passengers felt that a Wee Happy Bus, complete with cheery face painted on the front, might not have been the ideal choice of vehicle for such an occasion.

FROM a Glasgow minister we heard this story of the generosity of a showground family. He was called upon to officiate at the funeral of a member of the family. After the ceremony, the drivers and other employees of the undertaker involved each received a thank-you envelope. They were surprised but none too delighted to discover on opening them later that the envelopes contained a complimentary ticket for a ride on the ghost train.

OUR report on the moving and uplifting service for Norman Buchan, the Labour MP, prompted a number of readers to tell us how they wanted to go, when they had to go. Music was, of course, important:

Alan Ward, a Cambuslang minister,

recalled a parishioner at a previous kirk who left instructions for two good old Scots songs to be played at his funeral service. The coffin was to be brought in to the strains of *Will Ye No' Come Back Again?* His choice of music as the coffin was removed from the church was *I'm No Awa' Tae Bide Awa'*.

An organist at an unnamed West Coast crematorium passed on some recent requests. They included *Old Shep* (for a dog lover), David Bowie's *Starman*, and *Stranger In Paradise*. The organist was also asked to play the evangelical hymn *Colours Of Day* which includes the line 'Light up the fire and let the flames burn . . . ' Entirely appropriate for a cremation.

Richard Easson of Tain told us that his father's grave request was *Raindrops Keep Falling On My Head*. 'Unfortunately, we couldn't get the Sacha Distel version,' he said.

Smoke Gets In Your Eyes received more than one nomination as the tune to end the cremation service, as did *Keep The Home Fires Burning*. John Lennon's *Imagine* appeared to be the anthem for the sixties generation. Another sixties person, Robert Callandar of Glasgow, had an unusual choice for his musical crème de la crematorium. Mr C let it be known that, despite the fact he is a big lad, he has every confidence in the ability of his male siblings to cart his coffin down the aisle. He has chosen the Hollies' *He Ain't Heavy, He's My Brother* as the accompanying music.

Other gravest hits included Gracie Fields's *Wish Me Luck As You Wave Me Goodbye*, Eddie Cochran's *Three Steps to Heaven* for the deceased who has led a blameless life, and Chuck Berry's *No Particular Place To Go* for the person who does not believe in life after death.

And for a farewell to your friendly income tax or VAT inspector, how's about *The De'il's Awa' wi' the Exciseman*.

An anonymous football fan wished to be dispatched to the strains of *Cheerio, Cheerio, Cheerio*. But not everyone wanted to make their funeral a modern, upbeat event.

An artist of the Diary's acquaintance has decreed that when his time comes he wishes to be laid to rest on a faraway hillside. Inaccessible by road. The mourners will have to take turns carrying the coffin. In the pouring rain. Then they will sing all of Psalm 119 which runs to 176 verses.

'If I'm not having any fun, they're not having any fun,' is his logic.

And, by the way, there will be no women at the graveside. They will be back home preparing the boiled ham and the rest of the purvey.

GRACE

The subject of the humble Grace Before Meals produced a small but rich correspondence in the Diary:

WE have all heard of the Selkirk Grace but one which could rival it is the Langholm Grace brought to our attention by a local minister who has been introducing the victuals in these terms:

All creatures that on earth do dwell,
Wrax oot your haun' and help yoursel'.

A number of other Graces subsequently arrived in the Diary's mailbag including:

Holy, holy, roon' the table
Eat as much as you are able
Eat muckle, pooch nane
Holy, holy. Amen.

And the variation:

Roly, poly round the table
Eat as much as you are able
If you can, eat the table.
Roly, poly. Amen.

Then there was the extremely couthy:

Ye'r at yer auntie's sae don't be blate,
There's halesome fairin' on ilka plate.
Meat fit for provost, laird or loon.
When ye'r fu' as a puggy, lick the spoon.

Or the more direct blessing:

Doon wi' yer heid
Up wi' yer paws
Thank the guid Lord
For the use o' yer jaws.

The humble potato came in for special treatment:

O Lord wha blest the loaves and fishes
Look doon upon these twa wee dishes,

An' tho' the tatties be but sma'
Lord mak them plenty for us a';
But if oor stomachs they do fill,
'Twill be another miracle.

Then there is the special grace for anglers:

Guid Lord, wha gars the bonnie
*   specklin' troot.*
Loup tae our flees in loch an' river,
Grant us Thy grace, oor humble wish,
Tae Thee be praise an' glory ever.

THE Rangers football club has its own pre-prandial prayer:

Lord, heap blessings on the soup,
Heap blessings on the stovies.
Heap blessings on the Papes and Jews

The Moslems and Jehovies.
Heap blessings on all gathered here,
On absent friends and strangers.
And, if you've blessings left,
Please, heap them on the Rangers.

THE Scottish Medical Students Grace is admirably short:

For God's sake, fa' tae.

WE finish with the Aberdeenshire Grace:

God be wi' ye a' yer days
Plenty mate and plenty claes,
A timmer cup and a hoarn spoon
An ae tither tattie when tither's done.

GREENOCK

Greenock won a special place in the Diary's heart because of the rich and varied tapestry of human experience woven daily at the local sheriff court, all of it graphically reported in the excellent court columns of the *Greenock Telegraph*. The first case below proved to be the first of many:

He turned towards the person standing

Some place Port Glasgow, as can be seen from this extract from a court report which appeared in the *Greenock Telegraph* under the heading 'SAUCE BOTTLE ATTACK VICTIM NEEDED 34 STITCHES':

'MRS Myra Rancier (36) told the court there had been an argument and Brownlie had punched Mrs Findlay, knocking her over a chair.

'But she admitted she had not seen everything that had happened as she was blind in one eye, was drinking super lager and had been reading *Bunty* comics at the time.'

STEAK PIE FEATURES IN ASSAULT. The accused entered a chip shop in Gourock holding a steak pie. He 'stood in front of customers and demanded four pickled onions . . .

behind him in the queue and asked, "What are you smiling at?" and struck the man with his right hand which was holding the steak pie.' The man was found guilty of breach of the peace and fined £75.

THE Diary discovered a fellow student of Greenock life in Mr Iain Talman of Cardross. Mr Talman, a Gourockian by birth, has been collecting Greenock lore for many years.

He has amassed a rich collection of wee stories from the local courts, some of which suggest that Greenockians are not expert at escaping from the scene of the crime:

- **The passer-by** who was assaulted by a man who had emerged from a coin-operated photo kiosk. The assailant left his victim with wounds requiring four stitches to

his scalp. He also left four photographs of himself which were discovered after he had made his escape. The accused, thus, was the first person in history to leave behind a perfect photofit for the police. He was caught and fined £30.

- **The burglar** who found his haul too heavy to carry and went to the neighbour of his victim to phone for a taxi.

ALIBIS and pleas in mitigation can also leave a little to be desired, like:

- **The accused** on a drunk and disorderly charge who explained that he had been celebrating his birthday. This did not impress the bailie who checked the date of birth on the charge sheet which showed the man had been celebrating a month too early.

- **The bramble pickers** – two men found on a railway line with a bag containing a large quantity of copper wire claimed they found it while picking brambles. The depute fiscal somewhat spoiled their story by pointing out that the incident occurred in July, a time when there were no brambles.
- **The man** convicted of assault with a bottle who explained that he had consumed 17 bottles of wine that day.
- **The accused** on a breach of the peace charge who claimed he was being chased along the street by animals who were 20ft high, 7ft wide, and were breathing steam. His agent added that he was further upset because he had discovered his divorced wife in bed with an Englishman. 'I'm not sure whether it was because she was in bed with another man or because he was an Englishman.'
- **A young Greenockian** succumbed to temptation, as he stood in a chemist shop, by the charity Christmas stocking bulging with cash. He grabbed it and made his getaway. Police were waiting for him when he returned home with his booty. He really should not have been so surprised. They got his name and address from the prescription which he had taken to the chemist.

OTHER forms of behaviour which have led Greenockians into court are merely inexplicable, including:

- **The shoplifter** who stole a tin of dog food but had no dog.
- **The woman** who appeared in court to represent her husband on a wife-beating charge.
- **A youth** who was fined £20 for punching and kicking a litter bin and shouting 'Come on and fight'. The fiscal commented: 'He was presumably doing this because he knew that it couldn't retaliate.'
- **The man** who was arrested in a shop hitting his head against the walls and floor. This last-mentioned chap also assaulted a shop assistant with a packet of biscuits

and therefore qualified for the Greenock hall of fame for attackers who used everyday objects (see previous references to sauce bottles, meat pies, etc).

Other examples include:

- **The grandfather** who assaulted his grand-daughter in a supermarket with a shopping basket.
- **The man** who assaulted his wife and daughter with a TV set.
- **The husband** who stuffed an electricity bill into his wife's mouth. The accused told police, 'I just cracked up when I saw the bill and rammed it down her scrawny little throat.' (Greenockians have always had a way with words.) The defence lawyer said in mitigation that his client had been out for a drink and came home to find the electricity bill on the mantelpiece. 'It amounted to £130 for a period of six weeks . . . He feels his wife was the cause to a great extent of the amount of the electricity bill.' Sentence was deferred for six months.

THE Tail o' the Bank has a long tradition of unusual behaviour. Mr Talman's files include a story about a man who smashed a Port Glasgow shop window, stole a cloth cap, and was going to walk across the Clyde to Cardross. That was in 1885. *Plus ça change.*

Other famous Tail o' the Bank cases soon came to light:

A 70-year-old man was found guilty of stabbing his son with a bread knife, causing a six-inch deep wound. The father explained that he was trying to establish from his son the whereabouts of his wife. He said he went to the kitchen to get the knife 'just like a father taking a strap to his child' to frighten him into telling the truth.

A man who lit fires in a close and two litter bins was caught walking along the street with two matches in his hand and another two in his mouth. When cautioned he said, 'there was no malice to hurt people . . . They were just wee bonfires like Guy Fawkes did – wee beacons to warn people like they did with the Spanish Armada.'

In the midst of all this surrealism in Greenock Sheriff Court, there is the wise and witty figure of Sheriff J. Irvine Smith. Sheriff Smith recently had to take the case of a well-known persistent offender who seems to prefer prison to life in Greenock.

Sheriff Smith looked up to see the accused, who exhibits definite camp characteristics, in the dock and said: 'Oh, no. Not you again.'

'Well, who were you expecting? Joan Crawford?' came the reply.

Meanwhile, the *Greenock Telegraph* embarked upon the traditional circulation drive which involved a member of staff walking the boulevards and promenades of the Tail o' the Bank looking for people carrying copies of the newspaper. His happy task was to ask the reader a simple question and then hand over a fiver. The young man charged with the task had an unfortunate start when he spotted a comely young lady carrying a copy of the paper. 'How would you like to earn a fiver?' he asked her. Before he had the chance to pose the simple question, she rewarded him with a hefty slap in the face.

BUT in the end the Diary discovered in its researches that Greenock is not without gentility and class.

Two well-to-do ladies of the select West End part of town were not impressed when they saw in their local paper that they had been the victims of chip pan fires.

One of the irate ladies telephoned the paper and informed reporting staff that she had not been using a chip pan. It was, as she told them in no uncertain terms, 'a deep fat fryer'.

The other good lady felt she had even greater ground for complaint, for, as she told them, she had been making coq-au-vin at the time.

INSULTS

A reference in the Diary to somebody in the Sarry Heid pub having a face like a melted wellie, led a reader to speculate that the West of Scotland is richer in such descriptive facial phrases than any other region. The Diary was immediately submerged with many examples . . .

- A face like a hauf-chewed caramel.
- A face like a torn melodeon with the tune hinging oot.
- A face like a City Bakeries Hallowe'en cake.
- A face like a well-skelped erse.
- A face like a bag of spanners.
- A face like a burst couch.

77

- A face like a can of angry worms.
- A face like the hin' end o' a bus.
- A face you could chop sticks with.
- A face like a blind cobbler's thumb.
- A face like someone had set it on fire and put oot the flames wi' a shovel.
- A face like a ragman's trumpet.
- A face like a battered fart.
- A face like a robber's dog.
- A face like a horse in a huff.
- A face like a pudding supper wi' the jaundice.
- A face like a fish supper looking for a vinegar bottle.

- A face that has worn out three bodies.
- A face only a mother could love.
- A rerr face for hauntin' hooses.
- A face you'd never get tired of kicking.
- A face like a rivet-catcher's glove.
- A face like a torn kit-bag.
- A heid like a clootie dumpling.
- A splendid face for playing hide and seek.
- A face you couldnae mark wi' a pit boot.
- A face that wid turn milk soor.
- A face like the north end of a south-bound cow.
- A face that would turn a funeral up a side street.
- A face like the wrang end o' a Belfast ham.
- A face like a German bank – full of marks.
- A face like a sand-blasted meringue.
- A face like a chippit chantie.
- A face that would frighten the French.
- A face like a camel eating sherbet.
- A face that would get a piece at any door.
- A face like a relief map of the Himalayas.
- A face as long as Leith Walk.
- A face like a pun' o' knitted mince.

A WELL-KNOWN Hallowe'en game is often used to describe facial characteristics, as in: 'He looked as if he'd been dookin' for apples in a hot chip pan.' Or, of someone with a ruddy complexion: 'He looks like he's been dookin' for beetroot.'

AILEEN Fisher of Stranraer told how a ward maid at the Victoria Infirmary in Glasgow used to abuse nurses (including Ms Fisher) with the words: 'Your face would make a rerr Sunday arse for me.'

Telling comments from other readers included:

'If I had a face like yours, I'd paint ma arse and walk on ma hauns.'

'He was so ugly that when he was born, the doctor skelped his mother.'

'The last time I saw a heid like that it wis hinging oot a poacher's pocket.'

'If I'd a face like yours, I'd teach my bum to speak.'

'What're you going to do for a face when Quasimodo wants his arse back?'

'The last time I saw faces like that they were staring at me from a pirate ship.'

'The last time I saw an arse like that Sabu was hitting it with a stick.'

'He always reminds me o' a rat lookin' oot a jeely jar.'

'Is she ugly? If pigs could fly, she'd be a squadron leader.'

'If I had a face like that, I wouldn't bring it out on a clear night.'

'Tell me, is that your face or is your arse up for a breather.'

'You know – the wumman wi' the upside-doon legs.'

THE Diary gave an honourable mention and wee prize to one Phil McGhee for his suggestion of 'a face like a scorpion's arse'. It was not exactly in the rib-tickling class, but the Diary had never had a competition entry before from an untried prisoner in D Hall of Barlinnie.

THE editor of the Diary himself was not immune to physiognomical insult. Some ★★★★★★ suggested: 'A face like that man who writes the *Herald* Diary.' Another wit suggested that the picture which adorned the column looked 'like a werewolf peering over a dyke'.

YOU may also have heard of the Glasgow man who was so ugly as a child that strange men used to give him sweets to get out of their car.

KILWINNING

The nomination of Kilwinning as Ayrshire's Burgh of Culture came from a resident of the town itself and he must therefore take any blame for the Diary's famous list of anecdotes.

The reader was making the point that no Kilwinningites seemed ever to win prizes in Diary competitions, the implication being that they were perhaps not the smartest chaps in the West. Our correspondent cited a few examples of Kilwinningspeak:

THERE was the local man who complained to his MP that his name wasn't on the town's war memorial. This was unfair he felt, since he had fought longer in the war than his brother whose name *was* on the memorial. This led certain local cynics to ask him: 'Settle an argument. Was it you or your brother that was killed in the war?'

A KILWINNING man decided to take the train to Glasgow for the day. Asked how he had enjoyed his first visit to the big city, he replied: 'It's brilliant – and ah didnae know it was a' under gless.'

ANOTHER Kilwinning man was having his parentage discussed. 'Naw, she's no' his mither. She's his auntie. She hid him tae a sojer during the war.'

TWO chaps were having a drink in their local Kilwinning tavern. They ordered up another round of one pint of heavy and one of lager. The barmaid put the pints in front of them, but the wrong way round. The two broke off their conversation, stared in a puzzled fashion at the two pints, and then changed seats.

A KILWINNING chap won the pools. Asked in the pub what he would do with his winnings, he said he would buy his mother a house, his sister a car, and (being a Catholic, unusual we know in Kilwinning) he 'would like tae pit in a windae at the chapel'. A fellow Kilwinningite (not of the same persuasion) said that for £20 he would 'pit in a' the windaes at the chapel'.

THE following tale of Kilwinning Protestant intransigence was sworn to be true by a Glasgow University student who says he was there at the time. He was invited by a fellow student to a party in Ayrshire's Burgh of Culture. Having arrived within the burgh limits, the students stopped their car and asked a local for directions.

The Kilwinningite peered into the car and asked: 'Ony papes in this caur?'

'Certainly not,' was the reply although there was at least one.

'Are you sure?' came the rejoinder. 'Mind you, it's hard to tell the difference. They look mair and mair like us.'

TWO Kilwinning men, serving with Monty in his desert campaign against the Germans, were in a foxhole doing their best to shelter from the relentless sun. 'Here, d'ye ken whit day it is the day?' asks one.

'Naw. Whit day is it the day?' his pal replies.

The first chap explains that it is Marymass Day, the big gala day in the area.

'They've got a grand day for it,' the second man says, peering up at the cloudless skies.

Another Kilwinningite claimed to have been at the annual Marymass festival 'hunners o' times'.

TWO Kilwinningites on a night out to Kilmarnock missed the last bus home. Being lawless types, they decided that instead of walking home they would break into the Western SMT garage and steal a bus. One climbed over the wall while the other kept watch. After 15 minutes had elapsed with no sign of his pal, the man keeping watch shouted over the wall: 'Whit's keepin' ye?'

'Ah canny find a bus that says Kilwinning oan it,' he explained.

'Ya idiot,' says his pal. 'Take wan that says Irvine oan it and we'll walk the rest.'

A GREYHOUND in transit in a British Rail guard's van escaped on arrival at Kilwinning station. A Kilwinning BR employee chased the beast up the platform uttering the immortal words: 'Stoap that dug! It's a parcel!'

THE licensee of a Kilwinning hostelry noted for its unswerving support for things red, white and blue, had prepared for the next day's Orange Walk by painting a large slogan on the outside of her premises. It read: 'One queen, one crown, no Pope in our town.' To which a nocturnal graffitologist had added: 'Lucky old Pope.'

A CHAP enters a barber's shop in Kilwinning and joins the queue of men sitting. Observing that it might be some time before he is done, he seeks to pass the time by reading. 'Excuse me,' he says to the chap beside him, 'are you reading that paper you're sitting on?'

POSSIBLY the cruellest jibe about the fine burghers of Kilwinning is that when there is an escape from the state mental hospital at Carstairs, the police immediately throw a cordon around Kilwinning. 'If they get into Kilwinning, we'll never find them,' an official is reputed to have said.

KILWINNINGITES have their own peculiar way of putting things. Half-day closing is referred to as 'hauf-shut day'. A bank holiday has been heard described as 'hauf-shut day a' day the day'.

A DIARY reader shared with us his tale of a Kilwinning colleague in the RAF. When the chaps in the barracks room were being more than usually boisterous, the Kilwinningite would chide them with the words: 'D'ye think it's ootside yer in!'

DR GAGE was a well-known medical man in Kilwinning in the latter half of the last century and played a part in the introduction of a new, healthier water supply. The new water was welcomed by everyone apart from one lady, who told him: 'Doactor, this new watter willnae dae.' Asked to elaborate she explained: 'It's got neither taste nor smell.'

Dr Gage's duties also took him to the local poorhouse, where one old lady complained about the quality of the soup: 'It's no biled right. Try this,' she said producing a pea from her pocket. The doctor duly popped it into his mouth and agreed it was rock hard. 'Weel, doactor, that's exactly how it came through me this morning,' the lady informed him.

A KILWINNING lad announced his intention to marry a local girl known to be free with her favours. 'You're no mairryin' that yin?' one of his pals said. 'Hauf the men in Stevenston huv been wi' her.'

After a moment's thought, the bridegroom, obviously something of a philosopher, replied: 'Och, it's no' a' that big a place, Stevenston.'

THE most famous hostelry in Kilwinning was the Winton Arms, a redoubt of Loyalism and Orangeism. Lily McCaffer, who presided over the Winton for many years, told the Diary there were so many stories about her and her hotel that she never bothered to deny them.

The story about the time she sent home a regular who was wearing a green jumper with the words that he 'should know better' for example. Or the tale of the honeymoon couple who booked in, left their suitcases in their room, and went for a walk: on their way out of the hotel, they asked what time Mass was the next morning; on their way back in after their walk they found their suitcases on the pavement. Then there was the priest in plain clothes whose identity was discovered, his pint confiscated and his money returned.

Lily said such things might have happened under an earlier management. But she admitted she never wore green 'because it's unlucky'.

OVERHEARD in a Kilwinning post office: 'Two stamps please. One quick and one slow.'

A KILWINNING social club installed a satellite TV system. The committee became worried that the dish, situated on a low roof, might be too easily nicked. As a result, they resolved to have a local tradesman construct a secure box over the dish. On a subsequent agenda was the problem of poor reception on the satellite TV system.

THIS tale of a Kilwinningite came from Mr W. B. Thomson of Kirkintilloch, who recalled the occasion of one of the last shows at the Glasgow Apollo. Jerry Lee Lewis was scheduled to headline the concert but had been unable to appear.

The box office was busy issuing refunds, so Mr Thomson retired to a nearby pub where he found sundry disconsolate Teddy boys. Most disconsolate of all was a figure in a yellow drape suit, seated forlornly at the end of the bar.

W. B. related: 'I eventually spoke to him and it turned out that he had come straight from his work in Kilwinning, oblivious of the cancellation. I suggested, as a consolation, that he may yet see his hero at another venue, but he indicated that this wasn't a solution.

'"This is my effan problem . . . Look!" the Kilwinningite said, rolling up the left sleeve of his jacket to reveal the legend, freshly tattooed on his arm – Friday, 17 February 1987. Jerry Lee Lewis . . . His last show at Glasgow Apollo . . . The King Lives.'

Mr Thomson suggested the addition

of a tasteful 'Cancelled', but the Kilwinningite was not impressed.

A KILWINNINGITE was telling his cronies in the pub about his weekend's activities: 'Ah ta'en the wife oot fur a meal,' he said.

'Whit did ye hiv?' a pal asked.

'Stertit wi' a prawn cocktail.'

'Away, that's a wummin's drink!' was the reply.

We hear also of a young Kilwinningite who got a job as a barman. Remarkably, the young man was not versed in the ways of public houses, as he displayed when he said to the manager: 'The man there wants a pint and a half of lager but for the life of me I can't find a glass big enough.'

A KILWINNINGITE, telling of an embarrassing situation in which a fel-

low burgher had found himself, averred: 'Ah tell ye. His face was as red as an orange.'

WE were also told of a Kilwinning Rangers supporter's imprecation to a defender as a visiting attacker threatened the home team's goal: 'Kill him! Knock him doon stane deid like a lump o' iron!'

A VISITOR to Kilwinning tried to buy shoes in a local shop. 'Size eight, please,' he said to the assistant.

'We've went European. That'll be a 42,' she replied.

'They're a bit tight,' he said after trying on the first pair.

'We'll jist try an eight and a half then,' was her not very European but typically Kilwinning reply.

NOW, a story from Kilwinning's yesteryears. There was a fire at the cinema. A local by the name of Poison (so-called because he once had a poisoned finger) took control. 'There's a fire and everybody will have to leave,' he announced. 'And would you let the folk frae Fergushill oot first because they've got the furthest to go.'

THEN there is the tale of the stranger who asked for directions. A Kilwinningite said he couldn't go wrong: 'Take the first on the left and then doon the street, below the railway bridge that's no' there noo.'

LANGUAGE AND THAT

The Diary, as any reader would tell you, is dead into language. Thus, we are happy to offer a whole section on Gaelic, Lallans, English and that:

THE braid Scots dialect is usually to be found in the SNP's newspaper, the *Scots Independent*, or in letters to the *Scotsman*. But, in 1984, the magazine *Gay Scotland* brought the sonsy old words out of the closet by running a piece of fiction in the dialect. The tale concerned two chaps, Rab and Eck, who went 'fur a dauner intae the wuds'. The story contained numerous references to something called 'a moudiewart'. The *Scottish National Dictionary* tells us that 'a moudiewart' is 'a mole'. Obviously Rab and Eck were on some sort of nature trail. But then Rab related: 'We wis wuntlin a making a dirdum fit tae gar ilka mappie i the wud skeir stramulyert.'

A scene, we fear, we must leave to your imagination.

MUCH of the writing in braid Scots published by the *Scots Independent* was written by SNP activist Peter D. Wright. A typical article, of September 1984, said: 'At the hinmaist National Cooncil convene in Larbert, Athole Cameron richtlie myndit the Scottish National Pairty o the neid tae saufgaird and forder the culture, tradeetion and heritage o oor beloued kintra o Scotland. Agin the creepin Anglicisation, deed ay Americanisation alsweill, thare is muckle tae be dune tae mak siccar that a distinctive Scottish identitie is maintained.'

At least one fellow Nationalist disagreed. In a letter to the paper, he said: 'Peter's dialect is not authentic. No one in Scotland uses words like 'fremmit' (foreign), 'athel' (prince), or 'wittins-

blad' (which presumably means newspaper). This is just Oor Wullie langauge and an insult to the reader.'

Oor Wullie was not available fur tae comment.

A FARMER'S daughter, newly returned from university with a degree in English, was finding some of her father's ways a trifle coarse. After her father announced that he was 'awa' to scatter a wheen o' dung' she asked her mother: 'Can we not persuade him to say manure instead of dung?'

'Wheesht, lassie,' the mother replied. 'It's taken me 20 years to get him to say dung.'

THE Diary was indebted to Donald John MacSween, a speaker at the Labour Party's Scottish Conference in March 1984, for his help in compiling a glossary of trade union terms in Gaelic. This was in response to a statement by NUPE that the union intended to take more interest in the promotion of the language.

A toirt air bord, as you probably already knew, means: to take on board.

A toirt fa' comhair: to take cognisance.

Aig an deairbh am a tha seo: at this moment in time.

Neart an aonachd againn: this great movement of ours.

And, last but not least:

Dochason an luchd obrachd: the aspirations of the workforce.

A QUESTION in the entrance exam to Napier college's journalism course asked potential journos to explain what An Communn Gaidhealach was. One candidate answered: 'The president of Tanzania'.

ON a visit to the Outer Hebrides in July 1984 to take in the Feis Barraigh (the Barra Festival), the Diary increased its Gaelic word power simply by reading the programme:

Piobbaireachd le dram: licensed piping display;

Dannsa feillteach, einneir agus dram: carnival dinner dance with licence;

Bairbecuidh agus dram: licensed barbecue.

DOTAMAN, the BBC Gaelic programme for children, consistently gained a higher viewership than much of the rest of BBC Scotland's output. In particular, *Dotaman* regularly attracted more viewers than the channel's flagship politics and current affairs programme, *Right, Left and Centre*. The difference in the ratings had little to do with viewers' enthusiasm for the Gaelic language. The major factor was that *Dotaman* was presented by leggy Gaelette Kathy MacDonald who appeared in uniforms including a tight-fitting, whip-cracking, ring mistress's outfit.

SCOTTISH Television hired MORI to conduct an opinion poll to find out what the Scottish public felt about Gaelic broadcasting. The sample of nearly 1,000 people were asked if they spoke Gaelic; 92% said no, 4% said yes, and 4% didn't know.

AN English couple who had recently moved to Argyll applied to the local council to build a house. They intended to call the house Tigh na Botan. The Gaelic-speaking officials pointed out that this was not a good idea, since the name translated as House of the Penis. Perhaps they could try Tigh na Batain or Boat House, as they actually meant to call it.

A PRINCE Charles Gooder English Award went to whoever penned an advertisement in which Dundee District Council sought to recruit a press and information officer. It began: 'Due to the waygoing of the present post-holder, a vacancy has arisen for a press and information officer, which post was created to meet the changing needs in respect of the provision of information to the press and general public . . .'

No, experience with a quill pen was not required.

IN these days of sensitivity in matters of race, the colour nigger brown is no more. A Diary correspondent reported

that this shade has been replaced on colour charts by something called African Flesh. Doesn't have the same ring to it somehow. Can you imagine your granny popping into Trerons for a pair of African Flesh gloves?

A TALE from Furryboots City. (Aberdeen, of course. 'Furryboots are ye fae, yersel'?)

A visitor to those north-eastern parts told how he attended a social evening in which part of the entertainment was an Elvis Presley look-and-soundalike competition.

One of the contestants appeared initially to be in with a great chance. The rhinestone-studded white suit, the snake-hipped movement, and that mean, bad-boy sneer.

It's a shame that he had to spoil it with his rendition of *Blue Suede Shoes*, which began: '*Yin for the money, twae for the show . . .*'

MALAPROPAGATION

The Diary, with its abiding interest in the use of language, was pleased to begin a wide-ranging dialogue on Malapropism and Misspeak:

AMONG items received for the Diary archives were the Collected Pearls of Wisdom of a chap called Bill, recently retired from a certain department of Glasgow District Council.

Bill was fond of saying that since he began in the business there has been 'a lot of washing under the bridge'.

When the time came to go metric, Bill remarked: 'OK, I'm willing to go metric – 44 millimetres, aye that's nearly an inch.'

Bill had enough 'savvy flerr' when it came to office politics to conclude difficult transactions with the words, 'Have you got that in writing – no, well, I didn't say it.'

Bill was a great man for separating

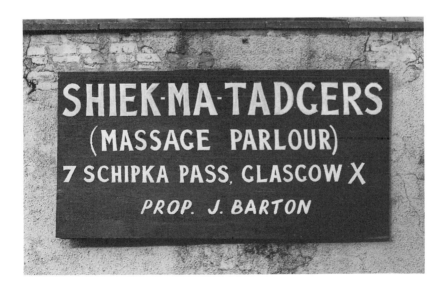

'the dross from the rubble'. After a particularly busy day Bill would claim to be 'fragmented out of his mind' or occasionally 'feeling like a well-skelped rabbit'. Sometimes he 'didn't know if he was on foot or on horseback'.

After such a day, and if the pay cheque was in, he would go to the pub for a few 'Glen Fillets' and would return to say the pub was so busy 'there wasnae room tae swing a dug'.

Bill was never a man 'to kill the fatted goat'. He would talk about his favourite sport of golf and compare his three-wood to his driver. One was like using a rapier, the other a cutlet.

Bill would discuss the news of the day saying wasn't it terrible that story in the paper about the poor cyclist 'who had had his leg decapitated'.

He would always find time to telephone his wife at home, once with the famous words: 'Is that you sitting with your feet on the mantelpiece warming your bum at the fire . . . Oh sorry, Mrs, wrong number.'

THERE were obviously a lot more people about like Bill. Joining him in the hall of fame was the manager (anonymous) of a factory in one of the new towns who warned during a dispute: 'Any more trouble and I'll be up these stairs like a ton of bricks.' On another occasion he told the girls in the office he wanted them 'to do the infantry'.

He mentioned once that a colleague had a big, new car with a venereal roof. And said of a noted ladies' man: 'He fancies himself as a bit of a Juan Fangio.'

As our informant wrote: 'That's it in a nutmeg. I would appreciate anonymity as the man concerned is still going strong and he would not be enamelled about this.'

FROM Carluke came the story of a lady who extolled the quality of the fruit cocktail drinks available at her golf club: 'Nice and fizzy with bits of apple, banana, and pineapple topped with a marijuana cherry.'

LOCAL government was a rich source of the pearl of wisdom and malapropism.

A councillor in Renfrew district opined that 'this item on the agenda is incontinent'. He also characterised a difficult situation by saying: 'We have buttered our bread and now we have to lie on it . . . '

This councillor also had a knack of handling public meetings. He invited a question 'from the lady at the back. No, not you. The woman beside the wee, fat, baldy man.' Needless to say the wee, fat, baldy man was not pleased and wanted to discuss the matter outside.

Another Bill-like figure worked in Glasgow Corporation some years ago. His pearls included:

- There are no flies in his ointment.

- He hit the ground with tremendous momento.
- His house was insulated on a top of a hill.
- When you get down to square brass tacks.
- He was illegible to join the club.

THEN there was this woman who went on her holidays to Pompeii. 'You know, the place where the saliva runs down the mountain,' as she told her workmates.

Or the shop steward in negotiations with his employers who said, 'We'll cross that bridge when it rears its ugly head.'

Or the woman from Bridgeton who did the Vermin's Pools every week and was a regular visitor to the Odious Cinema in Rutherglen.

BY far the most impressive submission of acrobatic *bons mots* was the list of 300 sayings uttered over the years by a certain unnamed production manager. (For some reason, most of our contributors on this subject wished to remain anonymous.) This gent's sayings included:

- I went through it with a fine tooth pick.
- It folds up like a banjo.
- Correct me if I'm right.
- Just let him stew in his own goose.
- He jumped in with two feet where angels fear to tread.
- That's me reading between the lines and making five.
- The rose is always redder on the other side of the fence from here.
- We're going down to talk roast turkey with them.
- He's had two runs at the cherry.

The problem was 'with all disrespect' that if the above-mentioned manager found out about this 'heads would fly'.

ALSO worthy of mention was the car park attendant at Glasgow School of Art who guided a lecturer into a space with the words: 'That's right, surr, jist park yer motor up there, paralyse wi' Miss Smith's.'

MR Rikki Fulton wrote to tell us that reading the Diary's malapropisms he laughed so much over his Corn Flakes that his 'treasure' came rushing to see if he had taken a fit. So taken was Mr Fulton that he has drawn the Diary's series of acrobatic *bons mots* to the attention of his old pal called Josie from the Coocaddens, who was famous for trampolining all over the English language.

Mr Fulton has forewarned to us a letter wrote by the aforeskinned Josie, part of which we reproduce below:

Sir,

I could not believe my ears when I conceived the Diary the other day in which Tom Shields appeared to disride the Glasgow patois. After all us

Glaswegians are already impaled with the heavy burden of their ethnic indentification because, admittedly, some of us do not metriculate our words properly and are at times, therefore, slightly incomprehensible. Need I remind you that Glasgow has been defacated the City of Culture for 1990.

For too long Scottish people in general and the Glasgow people in particular have been subjugated to the debilitating situation where they are not understood by the English, which is rich coming from people whose accents have to be seen to be believed.

Yours, Josie.

THE world of medicine provided its usual crock of examples, such as the old lady who phoned her doctor after five days of feeling unwell. Why hadn't she phoned sooner?

'Och, doctor, I've been treating masel' wi' thae hot fornications.'

Almost medical was the man described in court as acting 'in loco placentas'.

OTHER highlights:

- The lady who wrote her own 'holocaust' will.
- The man whose 'arse didn't know what his left elbow was doing'.
- The employee whose company gave him a 'rail vulture' for his journey to London.
- The union negotiator who could not reach agreement on a certain issue and suggested that it be 'kept in a basement'.
- The tourist asking the distance to a local landmark who was told: 'It's six miles as the cock crows.'
- The football coach who spoke proudly of his centre-half who 'had shoulders like Methuselah.'

WE were told of the Paisley building contractor who became involved in a court action. When asked to comment, he declined on the grounds that, 'It's still quasimodo.' (We think he meant sub judice.)

Also the foreman who was determined to catch one of the workers he had long suspected of sloping off the job. The man, however, always came up with a convincing excuse until the foreman declared in his frustration: 'That yin's aye got a lullaby.' And the forewoman whose patience was stretched by underlings constantly asking trivial questions until she told them: 'Just use yer ain transgression.'

In the trade union section we had the shop steward who warned his colleagues to 'keep their feet firmly on terra cotta'. Another steward in the steel industry proclaimed that 'the men are bending their elbow to suit management' but that the employer 'kept going off at a tantrum'. He promised his fellow workers that if they didn't win the dispute 'I'll eat this table without margarine'.

Then there was the chap at a highly charged meeting who shouted at a comrade: 'If you made a remark like that in Russia they would throw you in the Clyde.' Obviously, a pre-Gorbachev story.

THE office tea lady, according to the Diary mailbag, was a rich source for malapropagation. The gems included:

- My daughter's going through a difficult phrase.
- The company has gone bust. It's in the hands of the retriever.
- The doctor's put me on a diet. I'm only allowed that semi-skilled milk.
- A friend who suffers from cloisterphobia.
- A daughter who had spent nearly 24 hours in the labour ward: 'I wish the doctors would just hurry up and seduce her.'

EVEN those of us in the journalism business are prone to malapropagation. We are talking here of a news editor (anonymous) who inquired of a reporter: 'Is this story true or just a false herring?'

During the miners' strike, he asked one of his staff: 'Have you anything up your sleeve apart from the pits?'

When one young cub had his first story printed: 'I'm glad to see the penny's finally gelled.'

He once said to a photographer: 'Get them looking sharp-eyed and pony-tailed.'

He gave this memorable warning to the male staff before the arrival of a young female recruit: 'Her boyfriend does judo – in fact he's a black dan.'

TRAVEL was a fruitful area with:

The holidaymaker who went to Dixons to 'get a wee Mintola camera' and then couldn't wait to get to Spain 'to be back among the maracas dancers'.

The sad story of the lady who went to the Holy Land 'and had all her kroners pinched by a Greek peasant'.

The visitor to Italy who came back to regale his workmates with the story of the two founders of Rome – 'Remulus and Rolf' – who had been brought up by a wolf.

The chap who related his moving experience in Jerusalem when he walked down the Via Delrosa.

MORE MALADROITS: Some political malapropagation came our way. Hugh McMahon, MEP for Strathclyde West, was reported in the Euro *Hansard* as urging the European Commission not to 'go holusbolus, like a bull at a matador' on the subject of footballers' freedom of contract. Councillor Joe Reilly of Renfrew district was credited with this philosophical contribution to a debate: 'It's a question of dog eat dog and vice versa . . . '

THE polis received a number of mentions for the work of their 'plain-faced detectives' carrying out 'house-to-door inquiries'. Not to mention the time the 'mounted horses' had to take the field at the Scottish Cup Final.

IN the field of mixed clichés we have such sayings as:

- As happy as a sandpie.
- Above and beyond the call of nature.
- He had a memory like an octopus.
- He was born with a silver lining in his mouth.
- He had another kick at the cherry.
- She was like a lion in a corner shop.
- If you want to stand on your own two feet, take the cat by the scruff of the neck.
- I have plenty of other irons in the frying pan.
- He has struck clover and landed in oil.
- It was like a red herring to a bull.
- It was a minefield of opportunity.

MISCELLANEOUS MALAPROPAGATIONS included:

The fan who described the Motherwell football strip as 'clarinet and amber'.

The old lady who predicted bad weather ahead because of all the 'icy-bars' on the weather map. The elderly aunt whose sitting-room wallpaper had 'a gold pattern embezzled on to it'.

The woman who asked for 'partisan cheese' on her spaghetti. It was probably the same woman who remarked: 'I see they've found that listerine in ice cream now.'

The Lord Mayor of Belfast who commented that it would only take one coat of Durex to redecorate the Town House.

On the same broad theme was the woman who threatened her striking husband that he 'would get his conjuvenal rights when she received a full pay-packet'. Not to mention the schoolboy who described his father in his news book as a 'big balled man'.

OUR delve into the malapropagation mailbag took us to a greetings card shop in deepest, darkest Lanarkshire. A lady had found the wedding card which expressed sentiment she was after. It read 'Especially for You'. But it wasn't quite right. 'I'd like to make it for the both of them,' she said. 'Do you have a card which says 'Especially for Youse'?' Even in Lanarkshire, they didn't.

Also on the wedding theme, we heard of the bride-to-be who was too busy to go out with her pals because she was getting her 'torso' ready for the big day.

A Kilmarnock correspondent told the story of a local woman who was looking forward to her husband coming home from the Army on 'embrocation' leave.

Also mentioned in despatches was the young wife who liked to go on holiday and lie in the sun all day on her inflatable libido.

After three solid weeks of malapropisms one reader accused us of talking a lot of Pifco.

THE Malapropism feature extended to cover a whole range of life and language. A reader told how he was being shown some newly acquired paintings by a lady of the Kelvinside variety. He remarked on the Art Nouveau influence in one of the paintings. 'Yes,' she replied, 'I'm very fond of his work.'

THE Malapropagation Mailbag included:

- The lady whose attic has 'a nice wee skylark window'.
- The man who resigned from his job with the words 'That's the last time I work here and that's it in a nutmeg.'
- The wife who said of her less than perfect husband: 'Look, ah know ma man's no' a plastic saint.'
- The young woman who wanted to marry 'an edible bachelor'.
- The woman who walked farther down the road to get across safely at the 'Presbyterian crossing.'
- The girl whose boyfriend got a job with 'the Customs and Exiles'.
- Two bad apples don't make an orange.

FOOTBALL commentaries were rich in misspeak and malapropagation. Like the commentator (John Greig, actually) who came out with: 'Celtic have taken this game by the scruff of the throat!' In another comment on his erstwhile Old Firm rivals, Greggy said:

'They're behind at the moment but you cannot underwrite Celtic.'

BUT, away from football, how about:

- The US senator who declared his opposition to setting up a 'nuclear suppository' in his state.
- The Glasgow (or was it Edinburgh) councillor who supported a grant for a cultural event because he didn't want the council to be seen as a 'load of Palestines'.
- The Strathclyde regional councillor who, discussing a particularly disastrous episode, remarked: 'What's the point of having a post-mortem on something that's dead?'

EVEN after three months of correspondence, the Diary's exercise in mala-propagation showed no sign of falling into a basement.

There was the conversation in a West Lothian pub on the subject of Mike Tyson, the boxer: 'See thae young guys, the black guys fae the gateau, there's naebody can beat them.'

There was the chap who was not too pleased with the behaviour of his neighbour's dog which was 'one of those big Dobermann Pensioners'. And the woman who was suffering from 'post-mortem depression' or the lady who had refurnished her sitting-room with 'a mocket suite and eucalyptus wallpaper'.

A girl at a Lanarkshire church asked by the minister how she was enjoying the youth fellowship, said she disliked 'all the clichés'.

Worried that he was not getting across to a young audience, he asked for further details.

'The clichés,' she said. 'All those people who go around together and never speak to the rest of us.'

An elderly aunt telling her coffee morning chums about the DIY prowess of her niece: 'Maureen is busy now poly-urinating her new wood kitchen cupboards . . .' Maureen, of course, bought her DIY materials at MI5.

A senior Glasgow district council official commenting on the security for the Pope's visit to Bellahouston Park in 1982 pointed to some nearby multi-storey flats and said: 'It's almost impossible to give complete protection. I

98

mean, just think what a terrorist could do with a Carmelite rifle from one of those roofs . . .'

FINALLY, on a parting note:

A six-year-old girl, on a wet and windy caravan holiday in Argyll, as she left with the family for more extremely fresh air: 'Oh well, once more to brave the elephants . . .'

A Glasgow man looked forward to retirement when he would buy 'a wee self-contented hoose wi' a couple o' yon easy-gaun chairs'. All this, of course, before he 'shuffled off the mortal toil'.

Two old ladies discussing the recent death of a mutual friend:
'It was all so sudden . . .'
'Yes, especially as she had her celestial count only three days before . . .'

NAE LUCK

The Diary, being the recipient of many a hard luck tale, usually imparted with more than a hint of *schadenfreude*, instituted the Nae Luck Awards:

WE are all, to some extent, lumbered with public expectations because of the jobs we do. Take the chap who had the embarrassment of being taken off the plane at Glasgow Airport bound for Manchester because he should have been on the plane for London. Mutterings of 'Mastermind? That'll be bloody right!' could be heard from the delayed passengers as the chap walked down the aisle of the aircraft. Nae luck for Magnus Magnusson.

THERE appears not to be much of a future in futurology. That is the conclusion one might reach after studying the career of Mr Robert Underwood, one of Scotland's leading futurologists.

Mr Underwood was a member of the

101

Any unauthorised person found tampering with this board will be liable to instant dismissal.

School of the Man-Made Future until it closed in 1976. He then founded the Nevis Institute, devoted to examining 'trends in cultural, social, economic, technical and scientific life in Scotland'. After publishing only two editions of its *Nevis Journal*, the institute ran out of money and closed down.

THE Imperial tobacco company ran a Cash Snooker competition in May 1981 to promote their John Player King Size brand. Interest in the £170,000 prize was intense. In fact, there were 799,000 winners who each received the magnificent sum of 22p. Many of the lucky recipients decided to keep their jobs and live the same modest lifestyle.

RANGERS fan George MacDonald was so annoyed by his team's poor form in season 1983-4, he threw away his £45 season ticket after only a third of the games had been played. It was found by a Good Samaritan who posted it back to him.

HERR George Binder sent a mailshot to sundry Scottish households promoting the North-west German state lottery. The weekly prize of 1 million marks was quite enticing but Herr Binder kind of spoiled it by adding: 'It is not just the high prize amount that is so attractive but also the great number of fat prizes and the fat chance of scoring one or more.'

A RADIO Clyde car left in the car park at Parkhead by commentator Ken Robb was broken into. Nothing was stolen, not even the radio. But the bad boys who broke in did change the channel from Clyde to Radio 1.

THE Government published a brochure to show that the National Health Service in Scotland was in good hands under the Thatcher regime. The design on the cover of the glossy, full-colour brochure featured a reading from a cardiograph. Unfortunately for a publication which purported to portray a healthy health service, the cardiograph reading showed, in fact, an atrial flutter, a sign that the patient was not at all well.

A NAE LUCK award went to BBC Scotland, who broadcast on BBC2 a performance of Berlioz's *Te Deum* from Kelvingrove Art Gallery as part of their contribution to Glasgow's Year of Culture.

A viewer who by chance had left running the Ceefax subtitle service on his TV set was intrigued to find flashing on to the screen during the *Te Deum* such phrases as: 'I can't stand any more of this . . .', 'Who ordered the bacon and eggs?' and even the information: 'Toilet flushes'.

The technical hitch on this occasion was that BBC2 viewers in the rest of Britain were watching *The Mosquito Coast*, a film starring Harrison Ford, and there was no way of Scotland opting out of the Ceefax subtitle facility.

THE Berlin Wall was a potent symbol, so you can imagine the excitement when Strathclyde Regional Council's architects department received a chunk of it through the post.

A parcel addressed to the chief architect of Glasgow, Strathclyde, arrived at the region's HQ containing a chunk of concrete mounted on a tasteful wooden plinth. An accompanying letter, from the Architekturministerium Ostberlin to the Lieber Kamerad Direktor said that the bit of concrete was a bit of the Berlin Wall.

It continued (in bad English): 'We think hopefully that such a small peace of the Demolition may part of a new Bridge between East and West begin, and that our Ministeries may soon be joined in a new Spirit of Co-operation as I am sure you will agree that the Architekts must be seen to be the Leaders of the Renaissance. I look forward to perhaps one day you meeting.'

Mr J. C. McDougall, Strathclyde's director of architecture, was touched by the gesture and wrote back saying that, as president of the Chief Architects of Scottish Local Authorities, he would transmit the message from East Berlin to his colleagues all over Scotland. He added that he was grateful for the sample from '*Die Mauer*' which he would keep for display in his office. He also duly wrote to the Royal Incorporation of Architects of Scotland and to the Glasgow Institute of Architects, spreading the word of the glasnost news from East Berlin.

Then, as Mr McDougall examined the letter further, some doubts began to set in. Why was the crest of the East Berlin architect department the same as that of the Royal Incorporation of Architects of Scotland? Then there was the date of arrival of the package – Monday, 2 April. One day after a well-known day of fun. The signature on the letter was then examined closely: Floda Reltih. An unusual name, even for a German, and what a coincidence that backwards it spells Adolf Hitler.

Yes, one of the better April Fool stunts. And executed with an architect's eye for detail.

DEFINITELY in line for the Diary's Nae Luck Citation was an unnamed Scottish soldier in the 7th Armoured

Division, over in Saudi Arabia during the Gulf war.

Before his unit was despatched to the Gulf, the soldier managed to get along to his local tattooist for an appropriate image to be etched on his forearm.

He was quite proud of his tattoo, featuring as it did a drawing of a fierce rodent above a popular generic title commonly used to describe our brave lads out in that hot, sandy hell.

The squaddie is not the only one to sport such a tattoo but he was singularly unfortunate in selecting a tattooist whose spelling was suspect. Thus he was forever condemned to be a Dessert Rat.

104

THE NAME GAME

When the Leyland truck company merged with the Dutch firm DAF, it took less than a morning for the rumour to spread around the Leyland Glasgow factory that the new set-up was to be called, with overtones of redundancy, Ley-DAF. This is the sort of stuff, folks, we spent 12 years gathering in our Name Game section of the Diary.

SIR Colin Campbell, the portly chairman of James Finlay, the Glasgow

company much pilloried by pressure groups for their activities in Bangladesh and other parts of the Third World, is known as Sir Cumference.

BUFF Hardie, a member of the hilarious *Scotland the What?* comedy team, is one who confesses to having a diabolical memory for names.

On one occasion, he was greeted after a show by an acquaintance whose name he had forgotten. He was about to come clean and apologise when the man said: 'Don't you remember? Stewart Park?'

'Yes, of course,' he lied. 'How are you Stewart?'

'No, no. Stewart Park was where we played football as boys,' came the reply.

IN the bad old days of trade union abuse of power, there was a Glasgow docker who had the nickname High Noon. He was so called because he was wont to exclaim to his workmates during elevenses: 'Tae hell wi' this, I'm shootin' at twelve.'

ONE of the great double acts in the history of the Labour movement was

James White, MP for Glasgow Pollok, and Ian Campbell, MP for Clydebank. Before they retired in 1987, after many years at the Westminster coal face, the pair were inseparable. So much so, they were nicknamed 'Semmit and Drawers'.

Fortunately, the 1987 intake of Scottish Labour MPs included another great double act: Jimmy Wray and Jimmy Hood. They were both dapper dressers and looked for all the world like prosperous car salesmen. They quickly attracted a number of nicknames, including the Two Jimmys and the Wray Twins.

A NORTH of England constabulary boasted a famous but short-lived name for its version of a special patrol group. It was called the Fast Action Response Team. The acronym alone fairly put the wind up local criminals.

MEANWHILE, the team set up by Strathclyde Police to deal with ice-cream van drivers who played their jingles too loud or were too liberal with the tooting of their horns was nicknamed the Serious Chime Squad.

THE Scottish Office unit set up to deal with the problems of the travelling people was given a shorter and altogether snappier name by staff at New St Andrew's House. They called it the Tink Tank.

THE Renault car company had a successful advertising campaign in which owners of Renault 5 models gave their vehicles pet names. Renault suggested such names as Speedy Gonzalez or Gordon (after footballer Gordon Strachan who takes corners so well). Inevitably, one owner, less than happy with his Renault 5, christened it Rusty.

NAMES of Chinese and Indian food establishments can often be uncannily accurate. A Chinese take-away in Dundee is called the Tak Awa. An Indian eating house in Rutherglen was ominously titled Curry Fever.

ANOTHER suitable trade name was: M. Pyre (Builders) of Glasgow.

A DIARY reader sent us this list of his favourite (genuine) company names in the Hong Kong phone book: The So Kee umbrella company; the Lee Kee shoe factory; the Hung Fat brassiere manufacturers; and the Wing King optical company.

GENERAL Accident had an agent in Sabah (what used to be British North Borneo) called the Fuk Hing Garage and Automobile Service.

A EUROPEAN agency to promote multilingual broadcasting was titled Broadcasting Across the Barriers of European Language. Or BABEL for short.

THE Ubiquitous Chip restaurant in Byres Road, Glasgow, is a constant source of confusion for the many visitors to the city. One official of the European Parliament visiting Glasgow (to study urban decay and poverty) spent all evening trying to find a place called the Ultimate Chip. Dame Edna Everage in his Glasgow stage show referred to it as the Promiscuous Chip. Glaswegians sensibly just call it The Chip.

THE strong ale made by Robinwood brewery of Todmorden, West Yorkshire, is called Old Fart. Topers will be relieved to hear that it is 'additive-free'.

BUT surely only in the West of Scotland would you find a public house called the Duke of Schomberg, after a German soldier of fortune who fought and died for King Billy at the Battle of the Boyne 300 years ago.

THE company slogan of Durex Products Inc., of Luck, Wisconsin, USA, is 'Working to be the best, not the biggest'. We should add that this Durex is not in the same business as the British Durex, but makes mining equipment.

FINALLY, a few choicely named individuals:

The manager of the Saudi Arabia office of China Airlines was a Mr Peter Pan.

British Telecom boasts a billing officer by the name of A. Dove.

The Institute of Refrigeration once received a lecture from an engineer called Chilman.

General Secretary of the Industrial Water Society: Sue Pipe.

The author of *A Catalogue of Everything Israeli* is Josephine Bacon.

Oban boasts a lawyer by the name of Robin Banks.

A lecture at Glasgow University on the subject of Black Sheep was delivered by a Dr Woollen.

Partick Thistle had a full-back duo called Dinnie and Kerr.

The Ugandan Deputy Minister for Trade and Industry who visited Scotland in 1989 was called Mr Aggrey Suit.

A member of the staff at the Royal Observatory in Edinburgh is one Dr A. Heavens.

The deputy director of the National Centre for Earthquake Engineering in Buffalo, New York, is a Mr Ian Buckle.

The director of the National Fish Bureau of the Netherlands is one Robert Carp.

Managing director of the British Beef company is a Mr Jeff Steer.

Organiser of a conference at Strathclyde University on global warming was one Valerie Flood.

A member of the staff at the orthopaedics department of Paisley Royal Infirmary is a Dr Cartlidge.

Head of the Scottish Development Department's rural affairs division is a Mr Richard Crofts.

Appeals co-ordinator at Edinburgh Zoo is Mrs Isobel Beevor. A hard worker, we're sure.

Writing on the subject of slimming in the magazine *Treating Overweight* was Dr Lean, of Glasgow University's department of human nutrition.

PEOPLE

The following are some notes and anecdotes on people who did not fall readily into the other categories of the book.

ONE of Scotland's great characters was the late James 'Solly' Sanderson, sports journalist and doyen of the Radio Clyde phone-in. His highly personal style of prediction and controversy attracted a large following. So much so that an advertising agency decided to use his character in a series of radio adverts. They approached the comedian Allan Stewart, who did a very accurate impersonation of Solly. Mr Stewart said it would be no bother and quoted a price of £200. At this point the agency had second thoughts. They approached Solly and hired him to be himself at only £50.

COLIN Bell has been hosting a morning discussion programme on Radio Scotland for more years now than we care to remember. He does it in his own inimitable, abrasive and robust style. So much so that his first series, *Taking Issue with Colin Bell*, soon became known as Taking Exception to Colin Bell. His second, and current series, *Head On with Colin Bell*, quickly became known as Sticking the Head On Colin Bell. Which is what many guests and listeners often wish to do.

WE could fill a whole book with stories about Mick Broderick, singer and bodhran player with the Whistlebinkies, but we will not pre-empt the big man's own memoirs. A shipyard worker, he found himself pursuing his trade in New York at the time of the Watergate affair. He was sitting in a bar where everyone was watching with quiet reverence their President assure the nation there was no truth to the *Washington Post* allegations of corruption and criminal activities. 'There will be no whitewash in the White House,' intoned Mr Nixon.

'Bloody liar,' intoned Big Mick, starting a bar-room brawl of the type usually only seen in bad western B movies.

We will leave Mick to tell the world his other stories, like the pimp in Harlem who tried to buy the Mickey Mouse clock Mick had bought for his auntie.

We will tell you, however, about Mick and the time he left a recorded message with a parrot. Mick had been for a few jars and decided to go for a few more with a pal. He went to fetch his chum at his flat in Byres Road. The chap wasn't in. Undeterred, Mick lifted the letter box, saw the mate's parrot and shouted repeatedly: 'Polly, tell Jim I'll meet him in the Curlers at five o'clock.'

Jim duly turned up at the pub at 5 p.m. 'Did Polly give you the message?' Mick asked.

'No,' said Jim, 'but the old lady next door told me a long story about a wild man shouting a message through the letterbox to the parrot.'

ALAN Hickey is a travel writer with a difference. He is author of a tome called *Europe on 10 Litres a Day*. The 10 litres is a reference to alcohol and, yes, Mr Hickey is an Australian. The Diary met up with him when he was in Glasgow to research a new edition of his bevvy bulletin. He said: 'While other guides give you all the bullshit about what historic houses and art galleries to visit, my book tells you where to get the best and cheapest pint of beer afterwards.'

Mr Hickey was impressed by Glasgow. He told us the only other place in Britain to match Glasgow was Haworth in Yorkshire 'where those Brontë sisters used to hang out. I had a beaut of a time there for months drinking beer and watching television.'

He took up the onerous task of chronicling the world's beers and bars in 1974: 'I was sitting on a beach in Goa sharing an ice-box full of beers with this Irishman. He suggested doing a guidebook called *Globetrotting on 10 Litres a Day*.' Mr Hickey doesn't know what happened to the Irishman but he has been an itinerant author and drinker ever since.

He practises what he preaches and consumes at least 10 litres a day. When we spoke to him he was having a quiet Sunday. He had had a few pints of lager and was heading off to write up his notes in his hotel room. 'I've got a couple of litres of Füstenburg and a bottle of nice wine that I remembered from Cyprus,' and which he had discovered in a Great Western Road off-licence. 'I've also got a bottle of very strong Swiss ale that I found in a pub in Hope Street. I'll pop out later for a few glasses of Guinness and Tennents 80/- Ale.

'I will be telling my readers Glasgow is the place. The tourists normally go to Edinburgh, but all it's got is that bloody castle.'

THE Diary met Kayah Thet at the Easterhouse Festival in 1983. He was a merchant navy navigator from Ran-

goon, Burma, who had settled in Glasgow 14 years before. Joe, as he preferred to be known, was a fully naturalised Easterhouse citizen with a council house, a wife, two weans, and a Giro from the Government every fortnight. What kind of job would he like?

'I want to be a racing tipster on the *Daily Record* like Garry Owen. I can do that job.'

How does he enjoy living in Easterhouse?

'It's no problem. And, by the way, it's nice to be nice.'

POLITICS

Politics, from its highest to its lowest manifestations (the House of Commons to, for instance, Largs Community Council), exercised a fascination over the Diary:

A GROUP of anarchist students at Paisley College were faced with a dilemma. If they formed a society with 16 or more members they would qualify for a £200 grant from the college student body. Swallowing their anarchist principles they formed the Paisley College of Technology Anarchist Society.

The next hurdle was that, to qualify for the cash, the society had to have a constitution. Anarchists are not too hot on constitutions but a solution was found. With a piece of political sleight of hand, they borrowed the constitution of the Sports Society and added a final clause which stated that no member was bound by any of the previous clauses.

GREAT political issues of our times: During a debate in 1982 on the Civic Government (Scotland) Bill, a small schism appeared in the normally united faction of Scottish Conservative MPs. Albert McQuarrie, MP for Buchan, moved that every dog over one year old must 'have a permanent identification by means of a code number which will be indelibly marked on the inside thigh of the dog. The code number would be the identification mark for the life of the dog and the number shall be inserted on the dog licence.'

His colleague Mr John Corrie, MP for Cunninghame North, put forward a counter proposal that every dog 'shall carry a permanent identification in its left ear placed there by the breeder, with indelible ink'.

While the identification idea has obvious merit, both suggestions as to the location of the number carried disadvantages. Looking in a Labrador's left ear could be almost as unpleasant an experience as inspecting the inner thigh of an unco-operative Alsatian.

Update: Both suggestions were rejected and both MPs lost their seats in the 1987 General Election.

THE Diary's prize for the best use of modern technology was won in perpetuity by Andy McMahon, the innovative Labour MP for Glasgow Govan. The nomination came from a colleague in the Labour movement, who phoned Andy to find an answering machine saying: 'This is Andy McMahon, member for Glasgow Govan. I'm sorry there is no one here to deal with your call. If you wish to leave a message, please do so after the tone.'

The colleague duly began to leave a message, only to be interrupted by the bold Andy saying: 'Oh, it's you.'

IN the 1983 General Election, Mr Kenneth Hill won the award for the most reticent candidate. Mr Hill, who lived in London, told the Diary that he would not be coming north to campaign in Glasgow Shettleston where he was standing as British National Party candidate. Why not? we asked. 'Pressure of business.' What kind of business was he in that was more pressing than a General Election? 'I am in the cleaning business,' he replied. What kind of cleaning? 'Windows.'

Then Mr Hill came clean himself. 'We have active candidates and inactive candidates in the party. I am an inactive candidate, I will not even have time to help in the campaign down here in London. My name has been put forward with others so that the party will qualify for time on television.'

ROY Jenkins, before he was a lord and when he was fighting the Glasgow Hillhead seat in a by-election, went a-wooing voters at the university. A professor raised the topic of the number of Gaels in Partick. 'Oh, but the weather is much better at the moment,' replied Jenkins, who won the seat and subsequently became more *au fait*, as they say in Gaelic, with the Partick Highland situation.

AS early as February 1984, there was a campaign for a Scottish Assembly. And they had a plan for disposing of the 21 Tory MPs in Scotland. Of these 21 seats, 20 were held by a minority vote. If the opposition parties got together they could unseat all but one of the Tory MPs.

This is where the plan began to fall apart. The only Tory MP left in Scotland would be Bill Walker, in North Tayside. Despite the loss of seats in Scotland, Mrs Thatcher would still have won in the UK – and Bill Walker would have been Secretary of State for Scotland.

The plan was not proceeded with.

ESSENTIAL reading in any new edition of *Who's Who* is the entry under hobbies by Sir Nicholas Fairbairn, MP for Perth and Kinross. In 1977 he listed his favourite pursuits as 'bunking and debunking'; in 1980 it was 'giving and forgiving'; in 1983 'being blunt and sharp at the same time'; in 1984 'philantrophy and philogyny'. It has to be said that the entry for 1981 is a puzzling one – Sir Nicholas apparently lost his interest in the fair sex in favour of 'the cure and eradication of British tick fever'.

SIR Nicholas Fairbairn has turned in many bravura performances at the Commons. Like when he livened up an otherwise dull 1987 debate on devolution by informing the House: 'There are ten times as many Scots in Holland than there are in Scotland.' When parliamentary colleagues interrupted, he continued: 'Opposition Members who say "Havers, man" should consult the telephone directory for Schravenhagen to ascertain the number of MacKays who are living in that area.'

The Diary did not have the research resources to establish if Holland (population about 15,000,000) really did have more Scots than Scotland but we did have a look at the telephone directory for Schravenhagen, or The Hague as others call it. It contained three MacKays. It also listed a further 18 Makaijs, Mackaays and sundry other spellings. We cannot say, however, if they are real MacKays.

THE June 1984 Euro elections featured two lady Tory candidates with suitably European names – Patricia de Seune and Jacqui Lait. Ms de Seune, contesting Strathclyde East, used her name in her election slogan: 'De Seune the better'. The Tories in Strathclyde West thought about using 'All the way with Jacqui Lait' but dismissed it on grounds of sexism, plumping instead for 'Jacqui's best for Strathclyde West'. Neither was elected.

ONE of the matters of major importance discussed at the European Parliament in October 1984 was whether MEPs should be issued with a 'distinctive sash' (like those worn by French mayors) so that they would be easily recognisable at official functions. The design would be a circle of 10 gold stars on a blue background. Janey Buchan, the no-nonsense MEP for Glasgow, said she had no objections to Euro-sashes. But she did suggest one amendment – her fellow MEP Ian Paisley, no stranger to sashes, should wear his tied round his mouth rather than across his chest.

ONE Scottish MEP took too kindly to the European ideal and studied a number of foreign languages so that he could converse with his various colleagues at the European Parliament. He missed no opportunity to practise.

Dining in a Strasbourg restaurant, he was asked how he would like his coffee. '*Avec lait*,' he replied. The waiter did not understand, so the MEP elaborated: '*Lait. Le produit des vaches.*' Or milk, as the waiter finally said.

MRS Thatcher, on a tour of hostile territory in Glasgow city centre in September 1987, encountered artist John Taylor. Going about his lawful business, carrying a large canvas to his studio nearby, Mr Taylor found himself caught up in the street circus which surrounded the Prime Minister.

The Iron Lady pounced on him. 'Do you work here?' she asked.

Mr T replied that he was indeed on his way to his studio. This required a great deal of self-restraint since Mr T is an ardent CND supporter and his politics occupy a totally different part of the spectrum from Mrs T's.

'Can I see your painting,' she asked.

'No,' he said, making off before being captured for posterity fraternising with the enemy.

BELIEVE it or believe it not, life can become tedious for our MPs down at Westminster. It was boredom, and not malice we are sure, that led one to aver that it was his intention, nay ambition, when Cecil Parkinson was speaking to interject anonymously: 'Show us your willy!' This, being unparliamentary language, would be followed by the usual cries of 'Withdraw! Withdraw!'

DURING a House of Commons finance committee debate on the Poll Tax, Labour MP Brian Wilson complained that three Conservative MPs were reading books. The chairman ruled that books should not be read unless they related to committee business. Mr Wilson pointed to the Honourable Member for Crawley, Nicholas 'Bunter' Soames, with the words: 'He's not reading it, he's colouring it in . . .'

DUMBARTON is not fertile territory for the Conservative Party, as an advertisement for a secretary for the local party office indicated. The applicant 'must be a Conservative supporter and capable of working alone'.

BRIAN Wilson's winning of the Cunninghame North seat for Labour coincided with the publication of his book to mark the centenary of Celtic Football Club. Former Labour Party leader Michael Foot had seen a review of Brian's book and dropped him a note. Mr Foot said that he too had recently had a book published and suggested that both authors should swap copies of their respective works. Mr Foot's book was called *The Politics of Paradise*. Nothing to do with boardroom struggles at Parkhead, but a study of Lord Byron.

THE Diary suffered from an outbreak of political Light Bulb jokes in December 1989, in the wake of the Jim Sillars Govan by-election victory:

How many Scottish Labour MPs does it take to change a light bulb? Scottish Labour MPs don't change anything.

How many Scottish Conservative MPs? None. It's Conservative policy that the light bulb should learn to change itself.

Or, how many Scottish Conservative MPs after the next General Election? Both of them.

How many Scottish Liberal Democrat MPs? Sorry, we're too busy changing the party name.

How many Sinn Fein MPs? Two; one to change it and one to claim responsibility.

How many Democratic Unionists? Party spokesman Dr Ian Paisley said: 'Change a light bulb? Never! Never! Never!'

How many National Front MPs? 'We don't want to change the light. It's white innit?'

And, back to the chap who started it all with his Govan win: How many SNP MPs? Only one but he would have to ask his wife how to.

TOMMY McAvoy, Labour MP for Rutherglen, was sent a copy of the Bible by a Northern Ireland fundamentalist religious group, to mark the 300th anniversary of the Glorious Revolution. The Bible was adorned by a full colour illustration of a chap on a white horse who used to be king of Great Britain. (Yes, his name was William and he was Dutch by birth. That's it. No more clues.)

Mr McAvoy, an FP of St Columbkille's Secondary School, appreciated the gift but passed it on to some people who liked it even more. His local Orange Lodge.

JOHN Home Robertson, Labour MP for Berwick and East Lothian, wrote to the Leader of the House of Commons, on the vexed subject of English Tory MPs hogging the limelight at Scottish Question Time.

This letter, as is the usual practice, was sent to some faceless civil servant to concoct a reply that would cast the Government in a good light while assuring all and sundry that the principles of democracy were being upheld to the highest standards.

Unfortunately, by some slip-up, instead of receiving the usual anodyne reply, the Labour MP was sent a draft copy written by a civil servant and an accompanying note in the best traditions of the Civil Service.

The note, from a Scottish Office official to his Whitehall colleague began: 'I enclose a self-explanatory suggested form of words which deliberately avoids commenting on the figures he quotes (which are probably correct) . . .'

Yes, Minister, truth is stranger than fiction.

IT is not all beer and skittles, fun and games, wine and roses, for the delegates who have to attend the various political and trade union annual conferences from which the Diary derives so much of its material. Take this incident in the dining-room of a Dunoon hotel where the Scottish Labour Party were holding their 1990 conference. A number of STUC and party high heid yins were attempting to find sustenance after a long hard day, and the service was less than swift.

One of the diners was given a rare steak instead of medium. It was sent back to the kitchen for further cooking. Then he discovered that another diner had been given his medium steak in error. Doing his best to make life easier for the staff, he went to the kitchen to tell them. There he was presented with the sight of the steak he had sent back being stuffed into a toaster.

The whole thing proved to be too much for the chef/patron who came into the dining-room and harangued the trade unionists and politicians in the best Basil Fawlty style: 'You don't realise how much work is involved in cooking an à la carte meal for 17 people. My daughter has worked her bloody arse off for you lot!'

It was an interesting sight – some of Scotland's toughest negotiators gazing at their plates with nothing to say.

GUESTS at a cocktail party in Edinburgh Castle had an opportunity to see Mrs Thatcher in action socially. Herself and Denis were among the guests at a Scottish Office drinks and canapés bash to honour Scotland's Grand Slam rugby team.

Mr Thatcher, a former rugby referee, was in his element. Gin and tonic in one hand, cigarette in the other (even though it was a No Smoking zone) he was fairly enjoying the crack, as they say in Dulwich.

Then She Who Must Be Obeyed

appeared, tapped him on the arm, and turned away. That was the wordless indication that they were offski.

'Duty calls,' Mr Thatcher told the small group he had been talking to. This left the problem of what to do with the cigarette and gin and tonic.

There being no ashtrays, Mr T popped his fag-end down the muzzle of a nearby cannon, producing a nice little smoke effect in the process. The remainder of the gin and tonic he poured into some fake shrubbery which had been imported for the occasion.

Denis is a brave man if he does that sort of thing at home.

THE scene was one of the packed TV lounges of the House of Commons during the World Cup semi-final between England and West Germany. The game went to a penalty shoot-out. There were three Labour MPs in the lounge, all Scots – Messrs Dewar, Maxton, and Wilson.

The assembled Tories greeted each German goal with collective groans and each England goal with great hurrahs. A deathly quiet fell over the room as Pearce and Waddle missed their penalties. At which point Brian Wilson, the Honourable Member for Cunninghame North, was heard to say: 'Of course, it's the taking part that's important.' There was no reply.

A NATION ONCE AGAIN: Scotland's members of Parliament were urged to wear the kilt every day to their work. A letter to all Scots MPs said: 'We look to you, the elected representatives of the homeland Scots, to fulfil essential leadership roles in those matters of Scottish heritage and culture which are of special interest to us . . . Therefore, on behalf of the homeland Scots, all expatriate Scots, and all descendants of Scots to the nth generation, I respectfully suggest that you and all other MPs who represent Scottish districts, begin wearing Scottish national dress on a daily basis . . . '

The writer of this letter (yes, he was an American: one Curtis Hall of Cypress, California) said the benefits would be threefold:

'It will affirm in the strongest possible way the modern validity of Scotland's historic traditions and societal values.

'It will electrify the imagination and enhance the pride of Scots everywhere.

'It will instantly magnify your image as a leader of perception, maturity and character.'

What a great idea. We look forward to seeing Donald (Dewar) without his troosers, electrifying imaginations and magnifying his image at Parliament.

IT seems that the refurbishment of the Labour Party's image knows no bounds, with Donald Dewar emerging as a sex symbol.

An unofficial poll was conducted recently among Conservative MPs' secretaries and researchers in the House of Commons. The purpose was to identify those who were considered the most attractive available men in Parliament.

Donald featured towards the top of the poll. A member of Her Majesty's

Press made a few inquiries as to why the Tory gels should be attracted to Donald, who is more the bookish intellectual than the Robert Redford-style pin-up. 'He's very much a Heathcliff figure,' was one reply.

THE extreme fiscal caution shown by MP John Smith led to an outbreak of jokes in honour of the eminent Labour politician. It was apparently suggested to Mr Smith in the tearoom at the Blackpool party conference that it was his turn to buy the coffee. He agreed that he would do so 'as soon as the resources become available'

THE programme to root out male chauvinism in the People's Party has a long way to go. A detailed and laudable action plan was formulated to increase the number of women MPs and female party office-bearers.

This action plan was presented to a meeting of prospective parliamentary candidates at a Labour Party conference briefing session in which the MPs of tomorrow were being taught parliamentary and diplomatic skills.

One of the candidates showed he had not yet caught on by referring to the paper on women's equality as being 'as useless as tits'. This caused a sharp intake of breath all round and general pondering on exactly what he meant by this unfortunate simile.

The Diary was later able to establish that the full text should have read 'as useless as tits on a front-row forward'. The candidate, you may not be surprised to hear, was a Welshman.

ONE of the proud banners of the Scottish Constitutional Convention is the commitment to fair representation for women. Imagine, therefore, the shaking of heads which accompanied these remarks by Mr Harry Ewing, the Labour MP and joint chairman of the convention, at the close of a meeting.

Mr Ewing thanked convention administrator Bruce Black for his sterling work and also 'the lassies in the office who did the typing'.

THE PROFESSIONALS

The professions, notably lawyers and accountants, have been kenspeckle contributors to the Diary's ongoing survey of Scottish life:

GLASGOW lawyer Ross Harper, renowned for his persuasive pleading and witty ripostes, also undertook work as a part-time sheriff. Thus he found himself at different times on different sides of the courtroom.

During a case where he had appeared as defence agent, he asked the sheriff to let his client off with a small fine.

'Tell me, Mr Harper,' asked the sheriff, 'what would you do if you were sitting on the bench for this case?'

'I couldn't honestly say, your honour,' Harper replied. 'I have never been presented with such an eloquent plea in mitigation in any of the cases I have presided over.'

ROSS Harper advises young lawyers to finish their speeches to the jury with a piece of purple prose. It may not work, he says, but it is invariably good fun. He quotes one case where he had little to say about the facts of the matter: 'I decided to talk to the jury about justice and waxed lyrical if not eloquent. In conclusion, I held up my hands and said to the jury that as they passed into the jury room I was handing them the crucible of justice, and I made an offering movement with my hands.'

Imagine Mr Harper's surprise when one lady on the jury stood up to collect this crucible.

A MAGISTRATE at Glasgow District Court announced that, although the accused had been found guilty of shoplifting, he was prepared to take into consideration the special circumstances of the case: 'After all, the shop was called Kleptomania.'

SHERIFFS in touch with the lower orders: Sheriff Ewen Stewart is famed on the Northern circuit for his sayings from the Bench and excoriated on occasion by the Appeal Court for using material which is 'irrelevant' or 'based on his own researches'. However, the sheriff remained undeterred, as this quote from him on a case of a child being left unattended indicated: 'From my own experience in life, by nine and a half my friends had taken their tea badge at the Cubs, i.e. prepared the family tea for a week unaided; and I distinctly remember going home from school to an empty house on the servant girls' afternoon off when my mother was out socialising or shopping.'

LORD Jauncey, dispensing justice at the High Court in Airdrie, found himself overruled by a higher authority. The case had reached a critical point and, in order to make progress, His Lordship announced that the court would carry on beyond the normal finishing time.

Up spake a wee wummin from the front row of the jury: 'It's all right for you. But ah've goat ma man's tea tae make.' There was a strained silence while Lord Jauncey considered the situation. Would her man get his tea? Would the woman do some porridge for contempt of court?

Lord Jauncey finally spoke and showed that the qualities of mercy are not strained. He said perhaps the lady juror had a point, and sent them all home in time for tea.

THE reputation of Joe Beltrami, aka The Defender, as one of Glasgow's best-known criminal lawyers, follows him everywhere – even into his place of worship.

Big Joe was attending an Easter service at St Bride's Church in Bothwell. The service included a re-enactment of the Easter story. When it came to the point where Pontius Pilate asks the crowd whether he should let go Jesus or Barabbas, the distinctive Beltrami voice was heard to echo with gusto, 'Free Barabbas! Free Barabbas!'

When Barabbas was duly freed, there was an unscheduled comment from a member of the congregation: 'There's Beltrami got the guilty man off again.'

A WITNESS in Glasgow Sheriff Court was recounting in his evidence how he was on his way to visit 'two chinas'. The sheriff interrupted him in mid-sentence to say that he could see no reference in the case papers to any persons of Chinese extraction.

The same sheriff, inquiring about the income of an accused before sentencing him, was told that the poor devil had only £30 a week left after meeting fixed commitments. 'Why, that's hardly enough for a decent lunch,' said his lordship.

A SIGN in the corridors of the Court of Session building in Edinburgh reads: 'No offer, express or implied, of a contract of deposit is made in respect of articles left on these premises. No supervision of such articles is provided.' The Diary's claret-swilling correspondent in the black robe and slightly tilted wig translates: 'If you lose anything here, pal, tough luck.'

LORD Stott, sitting in the High Court, told an accused with a drink problem that on this occasion he would deal with the case leniently. But the accused was sent off with a stern warning to stay clear of the demon drink – 'including your mother's raspberry wine'.

AT the Appeal Court in Edinburgh, a man with five aliases failed to turn up. The macer left the court and called him by all of his five names. He returned to tell Lord Wheatley that 'none of them' had appeared for the appeal. The advocate-depute then asked for a warrant to arrest the man. Lord Wheatley, getting into the spirit of the case, asked: 'Is that for all of them?'

IN a murder trial before Lord Robertson at the High Court in Edinburgh, a pathologist giving evidence wished to demonstrate how, in his opinion, the victim had been strangled. Seeking a model to show how the murderer had grabbed the victim, the pathologist suggested he use the court shorthand writer. Lord Robertson said no, the shorthand writer was not a suitable choice. He indicated that Malcolm, His Lordship's macer (legal equivalent of his butler), would do, on the grounds that he was more expendable.

ROSIE Morrison, the colourful and comely advocate, spent three years as a magistrate in the courts of Hong Kong. During her term Ms Morrison was the subject of a complaint by a Chinese male. He was upset because, he said, he could see her breasts through her blouse. Ms Morrison was typically forthright in her reaction: 'My beautiful breasts which have given so much pleasure to so many! I was stunned. I said when they began to show through my tights I might begin to show concern.'

SHERIFFS IN TOUCH WITH THE LOWER ORDERS (Contd): An accused in a Lanarkshire sheriff court was giving a long and detailed account of the places where he had been partaking of alcohol on New Year's Eve. He told of various pubs and friends' houses he had visited and added: 'And I had a large whisky at the bells.'

The sheriff interrupted with: 'Tell me, who are these people the Bells?'

A GLASGOW lawyer was making something of a meal of his request to Sheriff Graham Johnston that the sentence imposed on his guilty client should be back-dated to his arrest. Sheriff Johnston, after sitting through the lengthy, not to say tedious, plea in mitigation, replied that as a special concession he was prepared to backdate the sentence to the beginning of the lawyer's speech.

WHEN the new Glasgow Sheriff Court opened on the south bank of the Clyde in 1986, a number of pubs and restaurants sprang up to provide sustenance to the legal profession. They had suitably legal names, such as Writs and Avizandum. Diary readers came up with their own alternative suggestions for naming a lawyers' pub.

They included Grievous Bodily Arms, Dunplead Inn, and Plonkers (this from a lady in the legal profession). Various drinks were suggested, viz: The Penal Colada, the Snowball's Chance (Advocaat and Legal-ade) and the Short Sharp Shock (a sixth of a gill). The winner of the pub name competition was Not Proven's Lordship.

SHERIFF Jackie Stewart of Airdrie proved to be one of the few sheriffs who tried to communicate with young people in their own language, often quoting from pop songs and other areas of popular culture. One youth was released from custody with a warning that the eyes of the law would be on him. If he so much as spat in the street he would be in trouble. 'In fact, just remember that you have Klingons on the starboard bow,' quoth the sheriff.

THAT enterprising law firm, Ross Harper and Murphy, advertised on TV offering a 24-hour, free legal advice service over the telephone. One of the male lawyers on overnight call was wakened from his slumbers by a call from a lady who proceeded to make

126

suggestions of a frank and lewd nature, with a proposal that the chap become involved in a situation which does not fall within the usual scope of a lawyer's duties to a client. The legal eagle, using a spot of the improvisation for which his firm is famous, replied: 'Hold on, madam, while I get the appropriate form.' Then he hung up.

THE law firm Bird, Semple, Fyfe, Ireland adopted the smart, if impenetrable, new logo, featuring a crescent moon and a sunrise. What does it mean? the legal fraternity asked. One came up with a suitably waspish answer: 'The firm has the sun and the moon, but no stars – and costs the earth.'

DONALD Findlay, QC, is a director and an ardent supporter of Glasgow Rangers. To his chagrin, his birthday falls on 17 March, St Patrick's Day. Fortunately, his pal, Glasgow solicitor Adrian Toner, who is of the other footballing persuasion, has a birthday on 12 July. An amicable swap was arranged.

LORD Wheatley, the first Catholic lawyer to rise to an eminent position on the Scottish bench, exhibited traits of honesty and sense of humour from his early days. As a young man he worked in the Glasgow law firm of Shaunessy, Quigley and McColl, a firm with strong associations with Celtic Football Club.

Celtic were involved in a Scottish Cup replay which was being played on a Wednesday afternoon. One by one, the senior partners announced that they were leaving for urgent and unavoidable meetings with clients. Just after lunchtime, young Wheatley rose, put on his coat and announced to the office: 'That's me off to Hampden as well.'

LEGEND has it that the town of Stirling once boasted a law firm by the name of Welsh, Robb and Steel. Glasgow firm McLay, Murray and Spence became known by jealous rivals as Delay, Worry and Expense.

ADVOCATES who come through from Edinburgh to ply their trade in Glasgow often have language problems, such as:

Witness: There was a chap at the door.
Advocate: And what was the chap's name?

Witness: So, ah looked at the clock oan the mantelpiece . . .
Advocate: I'm sorry, I don't understand. Who had been wearing a cloak?

Witness: Ah'd jist come oot the Vogue bingo . . .
Advocate: And what was the registration number of this vehicle, the Vogue Bingo?

THE traditional Glaswegian slovenly manner of speech can also throw your average Edinburgh advocate. One witness was relating that he had, at the time of an alleged offence, been in his local chip shop purchasing a soft drink and a packet of potato crisps.

What he actually enunciated was that he had been buying 'ginger an' criss'. To which the advocate said: 'Can we have the full names of these people Ginger and Chris.'

GIRVAN District Court was the location for this story, of a chap who decided to act as legal adviser to his brother, dispensing with any need for thae solicitor chaps. Hadn't you better get yourself a pen and some paper? he was advised by a court official.

So he asked the police officers in the court if they could oblige with the 'loan' of a bit of paper and a writing implement.

No, they said. As he turned away he called them 'bastards'. This did not go down well with the court. The surrogate legal eagle had even less luck in the afternoon session, when he returned refreshed and was arrested for shouting and swearing. He was fined £40.

As the local newspaper, the *Carrick Herald*, said on the matter: 'His debut as a "solicitor" wasn't quite in the Joe Beltrami league.'

AND another wee story from the courts . . . A businessman was responsibly but reluctantly performing a spell of jury duty. To his horror, he was nominated to be foreman of the jury. 'No, I can't be foreman,' he said. 'It should be Mr Smith.'

Why? he was asked.

'I'm sitting in the back row and the foreman of the jury has to sit at the front,' he replied.

His fellow-members of the jury were considering this dubious legal point when a lady piped up: 'Aye, that's right. That's the way it always is in *LA Law*.'

THE identification parade is a rich source of legal legend and controversy. (Just ask Patrick Connolly Meehan.)

We liked the folk-tale-which-may-well-be-true about the suspect in a robbery case who was in a line-up at the local nick. One of the witnesses asked if she could hear the members of the parade say the words: 'Where's the money?'

This the members of the public on

parade duly did. But when it came to the suspect, he didn't seem to understand what was expected of him. He said nothing. 'Where's the money?' barked the policeman in charge.

'It's in the hoose!' said the suspect – or the accused as he soon became known.

THE scene was Glasgow Sheriff Court. The charge was assault by stabbing. The procurator-fiscal's examination of the victim went something along these lines:

'Did something happen to you around October 1989?'

'Ah wis thingmied.'

'What were you thingmied with?'

'A thingmy.'

'So what you are telling us is that, in October 1989, you were thingmied with a thingmy.'

'Aye.'

'Can you tell the court where you were thingmied?'

'Aye. In the what do you call it . . . you know.'

Subsequently, a submission that the Crown had failed to thingmy their case was upheld.

WORTHY of a passing mention is the accused at Edinburgh Sheriff Court who, when asked how he would like to plead, replied: 'Not proven.'

A LAWYER at Glasgow Sheriff Court was trying to persuade the bench that an assault case should be adjourned until a certain witness was able to attend.

The sheriff was reluctant since the case had already been adjourned four times due to non-appearance of the said witness. What vital evidence would she be able to contribute? he asked.

'The young lady will testify that she made love to the accused 15 minutes before the alleged attack and she will state that at that time he did not have an offensive weapon in his trousers.'

A DUNDEE court was hearing a case involving a frozen outside a Chinese takeaway. Part of the evidence related to an item of nourishment which had been purchased from the takeaway.

'And what happened to the carry-out food?' the defence lawyer asked.

The witness replied: 'A' e' i' a'.' Thus becoming, possibly, the first witness in a courtroom to utter a full sentence without a consonant.

AN accused in a case at Falkirk Sheriff Court showed some skill as a pleader.

He had been involved in a fight with another youth. Despite the fact that they were both pleading guilty, his co-accused brought in the services of a well-known Glasgow criminal law firm. Our man decided to represent himself.

The Glasgow lawyer duly made a lengthy and eloquent plea in mitigation. Our man, when asked what he

GRATEFUL THANKS SACRED
HEART, St Jude and Blessed
Virgin.—P.C.

GRATEFUL THANKS St Jude and St
Anthony, Allah be praised.

HEATHER DEVONISH is 18 today.
HAPPY BIRTHDAY love from your
mum, dad and brother Peter.

had to say for himself, replied: 'Ah'm jist an erse.'

Both accused received the same sentence.

THE scene was a High Court trial in which an 86-year-old man was giving evidence about a robbery at his house. He asked if he could sit down in the witness box and the judge, Lord Clyde, agreed.

Lord Clyde then reminded him of the importance of the jury being able to hear him across the other side of the courtroom: 'Remember to raise your voice as loudly as you can, particularly when you are speaking.'

What you might call sound advice.

THE High Court in Edinburgh was hearing evidence about a fracas involving a number of men who chased their alleged victim into Tony's Café, an Edinburgh chip shop. The man was asked: 'What do you remember about events in the chip shop?'

'I was getting battered,' replied the witness.

THE Diary thought it had better preserve for posterity this rare event – a joke about accountants, told by an accountant:

An accountant is accosted in the street by a down-and-out.

'Excuse me, sir, could you spare 10p for a cup of tea,' says the beggar. 'I've had nothing to eat for the past three days and I've only had £3.50 to spend on food in the past fortnight.'

'That's very interesting,' the accountant replies. 'And tell me, how does this compare with your performance for a similar period last year?'

TWO accountants, equally qualified,

are on the short leet for a job. The employer asks each the same simple arithmetical problem: What is two and two? The first accountant said the answer was four. The second answered: 'It all depends. What would you like it to be?' The second accountant got the job.

COOPERS & Lybrand, the chartered accountants, took out a series of TV adverts telling people that they could be millionaires if they took advice from their company. The ads brought in a number of serious inquiries. On the debit side, one of the senior partners had the distressing experience of having to eject from his office a potential client, slightly the worse for an extensive liquid lunch, who refused to leave until he had, indeed, been made a millionaire.

READERS' WRITES

One of the features of *Herald* Diary columns over the years has been their ability to involve the reader. Some say that this is merely a way of having the readers do all the hard work. The truth is that the *Herald* readership includes some extraordinarily clever people and it is very much in the public interest that their wit be published.

The first competition I ever ran was suggested by colleague Roddy Forsyth. He noticed that the book *Six Days of the Condor* had been made into a film called *Three Days of the Condor*. We invited readers to come up with their suggestions for other half-frame

In the eye

I HAVE distorted vision in the right eye. Could the cause be something in my stomach?

No – it's something in the eye! Do seek your doctor's opinion.

films. These included:

*Snow White and the Three and a
   Half Dwarves*
The One and a Half Musketeers
Five (Hard Luck, Bo Derek)
Stereophenia
*One and a Half Coins in the
   Fountain*
The Three-and-a-Half-Year Itch
The Magnificent Three and a Half
The Slightly Soiled Half Dozen
Fellini's Four and a Quarter
Catch 11
Fahrenheit 250½

The winning entry was *The Wizard of 14 Grammes*.

The Diary was later inspired by Mayfest stand-up comedian Howard Busgang, who had in turn been inspired by Kurt Vonnegut's *Slaughterhouse Five*, to run a competition called Backward Films. In his act Mr Busgang related the plots of films which had been inadvertently run back-to-front:

The Godfather is a happy story about some really bad gangsters who gave up a life of crime to lead a simple peasant life in Sicily; *Friday the Thirteenth* is a tale about a nice person who goes

133

round pulling knives out of people and making them better. Using this back-track philosophy:

The Titanic is a film about a giant sub-marine which surfaces, picks up lots of people who appear foolishly to have gone swimming or sailing in rowing boats in the middle of the Atlantic, and takes them back to Liverpool.

Psycho is about this mental patient who overcomes his problems, rescues a girl trapped in a car in a murky pond, and cleans her up in the shower before she returns home.

Roots is a backward TV serial much loved by members of the Ku Klux Klan. It tells how prosperous and in-tegrated black people in American society are thrust back into slavery and, even better from the Klan point of view, are put into ships and taken back to Africa.

In *My Fair Lady* a wealthy London lady has an upper-class accent she wants to get rid of so that she can com-municate with the poor folk of Covent Garden.

The Sound of Music is an unusual tale about a woman who gives a bunch of children aversion therapy to music by teaching them to forget various dread-ful songs. She then makes curtains out of their clothes before going back to a nunnery.

It's a Wonderful Life is the story of a crooked businessman who cheats the people of a small town before commit-ting suicide with the help of an angel.

The Agony and the Ecstasy is about a Pope on his death-bed who apparently has an aversion to his painted ceiling. He hires a chap called Michaelangelo to strip the paint off. He then recovers his health.

Gone with the Wind is the story of a wil-ful young woman who averts the American Civil War, puts out a major fire at Atlanta, extends slavery to all the states of America, and leaves her hus-band for a wimp called Ashley.

Gregory's Girl, in the backward ver-sion, is about a lanky youth who likes to lie in the park in Cumbernauld with attractive young women. But he gives up girls to concentrate on playing foot-ball for the school team.

The Dirty Dozen is a sad story of Allied soldiers who fight their way out of a French château occupied by German troops. They escape back to England where they are untrained, put in prison and then charged with sundry crimes such as murder and rape.

A Bridge Too Far is another war story but with a happy ending. A whole army of plucky soldiers are surrounded and vastly outnumbered by the Germans. They retreat, doing repair work on any bridges they pass, and escape back to England by jumping 10,000 feet back into their aeroplanes.

The Graduate: A young man throws off the shackles of marriage to have a fling with an older woman, and experiments with rubber fetishism in his swimming pool, before going to college.

Casablanca: The chief of police tells his men to allow the usual suspects to go home. Rick goes to the airport to meet Ilsa. They sit around in a café agonising as time goes by. They part but meet many years later and have a dirty weekend in Paris before splitting up forever.

Fatal Attraction: A beautiful but impetuous woman is harassing a married couple by messing up their bathroom, kidnapping their child, and making constant phone calls. The husband solves the problem by meeting her, and taking her to bed, after which they part amicably.

Bridge Over the River Kwai: Alec Guinness builds a bridge by the simple device of pulling up the plunger on a detonator device. His men then laboriously dismantle it before going back to a PoW camp where they sit around with nothing to do.

The Ten Commandments: The Jews, fed up with Moses's strict laws, send him back up the mountain with the Commandments. His people stop having an orgy and decide to head back to Egypt where the Pharaoh is waiting for them. They are given council houses and celebrate by wiping the lamb's blood off the lintels. They get MSC jobs building pyramids and live for many a happy year by the Nile.

A Town Like Alice: An Australian couple go to Malaya with a Japanese travel firm. They fall out over the inclusion of chicken on the menu. She goes to live in England. He goes back to Alice Springs to be a shepherd.

The Wooden Horse: A hand-picked team of Allied soldiers tunnel into a German PoW camp, where they entertain the troops with gymnastic displays under the nose of the Hun.

Frankenstein: An ugly chap goes to a doctor for plastic surgery. Instead, the doc dismembers him and buries the pieces in various local graveyards.

The Cannonball Run: A bunch of crazy car drivers race backwards across the USA and it ends in a dead heat.

Guess Who's Coming to Dinner: A couple are having a pleasant dinner with their daughter's black boyfriend.

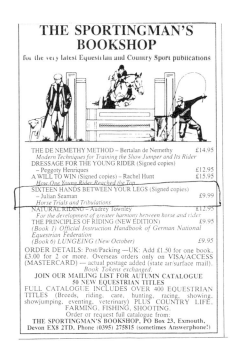

But he proves to be such a smart ass they throw him out.

Whisky Galore: The entire population of a Hebridean island decides to go tee-total. They search every nook and cranny of the island, collect every drop of the hidden hooch, and ferry it out to a beached freighter. The ship is re-floated and sails off into the fog.

Geordie: A strapping Highlander is Olympic champion hammer-catcher in Australia. He returns to Scotland to work as a farm labourer. He spends less and less time at the hammer-catching and eventually ends up emaciated.

The 39 Steps: Robert Donat is watching a mind-reading act in a London theatre. He takes off for Scotland where he steals a car, makes a political speech, and is shot. He leaps on to the Forth Rail Bridge, gets himself hand-cuffed to Madeleine Carroll, and goes back to London. There he dresses up as a milkman while someone is murdered in his flat.

Dracula: A gang of Transylvanian villagers led by a doctor extract a big skelf from a local gent's chest. The grateful gent undertakes nightly visits to the bedrooms of anaemic ladies, restoring them to health by means of blood transfusions.

Greyfriars Bobby: A wee dog is sitting by a plot in a graveyard in Edinburgh. The grave opens and a man (whom the wee dog obviously knows) emerges from the coffin. The man and dog go away and live happily ever after.

The Third Man: An American in Vienna rescues a fellow countryman from a sewer while on the way back from a funeral. The rescued man disappears. The rescuer gets fed up being harrassed by British military police and goes home.

Ice Cold in Alex: John Mills and Anthony Quayle meet in a bar in Egypt. They have a few chilled lagers too many, hijack an ambulance, drive into the desert and get lost.

THE idea of backward films led on to a wider examination of life as seen through a rear-view mirror. We had readers writing in with some very interesting Backward Concepts . . .

The year in question is 1988, and Celtic have celebrated their Centenary year by winning the Scottish Cup and Premier League double. Then things begin to go backwardly bad:

First they climb back up the steps to hand the cup and individual medals back to Mrs Thatcher. There then follow a number of football matches where the Celtic forward line keep running away from the opponents' goal-mouth and each game ends in a disappointing 0-0 draw.

Even more perturbing is the tendency of the Old Firm to take the field with only nine or ten players, with the missing players coming back on at different times during the game as the referee puts his red card back in his pocket.

The league season ends with all 12 teams in a tie for top and bottom places with no points and no goals scored. The Celtic board are obviously upset at this way of celebrating their 99th birthday and sack manager Billy McNeill in favour of Davie Hay.

Mrs Thatcher's career provided an interesting Backward Concept.

First she cancels the Poll Tax (this was pre-Major, please remember) in favour of a property tax. She national ises British Telecom, British Gas et al. This is paid for by higher taxes on the rich.

After eight years of undoing Conservative legislation, she resigns as Prime Minister and goes into opposition. She makes a comeback as Education Minister under Ted Heath. After reintroducing school milk for children of all ages, she demits ministerial office for the back benches.

She leaves Parliament to be a housewife. Her husband Denis leaves to rejoin his first wife. She goes to university where she has degrees in law and chemistry taken away from her as she begins to know less and less about the subjects.

There is a happy ending as she goes back to Grantham, Lincolnshire, to be the daughter of the owner of a corner grocery shop.

The Glasgow Garden Festival of 1988 found itself a victim of Backward Concepts.

Millions of visitors gradually drift away from the Garden Festival site. One day in April the Prince of Wales performs a closing ceremony. The trees, buildings, exhibition pavilions and even the very grass are ripped out. The Scottish Development Agency takes its £35,000,000 back. The site lies derelict for many years. Then a flourishing docks and shipbuilding industry develops.

Scottish industry, too, is very much a backward story.

The Linwood car factory re-opens and trains its labour force to dismantle vehicles. The River Clyde becomes the centre of the world's shipbreaking industry. The scrapping of some of the world's largest ships become occasions for royal visits as the vessels are dragged ashore.

The revitalisation of these industries is accompanied by a population movement back to cosier, if more crowded, accommodation in inner city areas. Housing estates in Castlemilk, Easterhouse, Drumchapel and Pollok are demolished and the land returned to farming use.

Meanwhile in Lanarkshire, Fife and other rural areas, large numbers of immigrant workers are employed to bury coal in the ground before being sent back to Ireland and the Highlands.

A SPOKESMAN for Lothian Fire Brigade started it all when he said that a blaze had been started by 'some bampot'. The Diary reported that the Press Association news agency had to put out an explanatory paragraph to the English media saying that bampot was a Scottish word for idiot. Diary readers, as they often do, joined in the debate uninvited . . .

A bampot was, in fact, a section of thick bamboo filled with explosives, said one.

No, a bampot was the bowl or receptacle in a dry toilet and a bamstick (another common Scots word) is the stick used to remove the aforementioned bampot for the purpose of emptying.

No, bampot comes from balm, an aromatic substance used to mask the smell from this pot.

No, actually, bampot was named after the town of Bam in Iran.

No, definitively, bampot comes from the brewing trade where the froth on fermenting beer is called the barm. Thus a bampot is one whose head is in ferment or full of wee bubbles.

A scholarly reader had the last word when he claimed to have uncovered a Scots verb, to bamp, which means to harp on constantly about the same topic.

WE suggested that the Scottish Prison Service's recently launched newspaper, the *Informer*, might have been better named the *News of the Screws*. Readers' suggestions included:

Time Magazine
The Daily Stir
The Indepenitentiary

Inside Crack
Daily Mailbag
Peephole's Friend
The Two-Way Daily Mirror

THE *Evening Standard*, London's local paper, irked the Scots with a readers' offer for T-shirts bearing the words: 'There is No Life North of Watford.' Diary readers were quick to retaliate with such slogans as:

Scotland Borders on the
    Uncultured
Stuff London Up Your Arsenal
Grow Your Own Dope – Plant an
    Englishman
You're Very Welcome to London
London is Full of Tubes
Live South of the Tweed? Yer Aff
    Yer Heid!
When the Germanic Tribes
    Invaded Britain the Acute
    Angles Moved North While the
    Obtuse Angles Went South
Living in London is Capital
    Punishment

THE rivalry between Prestwick and Glasgow airports led to a suggestion that the Ayrshire one be renamed Robert Burns International, in an attempt to retain the American tourist market. Naturally, the Diary readers got into the act by proposing a name change for Glasgow airport. Suggestions included:

Jean Armour International

138

Peter McCann International
Dalriada International Airport
Ally MacLeod Memorial
    International Airport
Greek Thomson Holidays Airport
Keelie's Landing
Jimmy International
Cheerio, Cheerio International
Stanley Baxter International (He
    does such good take-offs)
Doo Lally International
Rab C. Nesbitt International
Charles De Goal International
    (after Charlie Nicholas)
George Younger Memorial
    International
Jock Tamson Airport
The Just Outside Glasgow Actually
    in Paisley Airport
Wheech International
Itsyersel International (Edinburgh
    airport to be renamed You'll
    Have Had Your Tea
    International)
We Aero People International
Hudgie International
Erranerri Errport

There were suggestions that Prestwick's new name should be Sydney Devine Ayrodrone or Princess Anne International (because it is fog-free).

TO mark the opening in Glasgow of a smart hotel and bistro called Rab Ha's, after the famous Glesca Glutton, the Diary asked readers to come up with a CV which would make Rab more of a Yuppie.

Rab's real name, we were told, was John Robert McTammany Hall. He emigrated from Glasgow to New York, where he rapidly rose through the political ranks. He left New York in disgrace after consuming the entire purvey for the mayor's Thanksgiving Dinner. He joined the Confederate Army catering corps and was billeted at Tara, near Atlanta, where his cooking inspired *Gone with the Wind*. After the Civil War he took up a job as chicken inspector for Colonel Saunders. During this period he cured himself of gluttony by inventing an aversion therapy called cold turkey.

Rab Ha' was actually a well-known but financially embarrassed roofing contractor in Glasgow last century. Creditors who called at his various places of work were invariably told by his apprentice: 'Rab Ha's on the slates' –

giving rise to a famous piece of Glasgow slang.

Rab was actually the smallest of three brothers; the other two being Kelvin and Albert.

Rab Ha' was extremely fond of boiled food such as potatoes, fish and beef. He it was who came up with the slogan 'Glasgow Biles Better'.

Rab Ha' was actually a famous all-in wrestler. He competed under various pseudonyms including that of Garth (later to become a newspaper cartoon strip) and invented the Garth Arm Lock, a name subsequently given to an area of Glasgow. He was equally famous for his large appetite and was also known as the Maulin' Diner and had a burn named after him. His culinary skills were the talk of the city. He was the first chef to use Irn Bru in cooking – as a marinade for an entire ox. This Irn Bru Roast Ox (or IBROX for short) became so popular that a part of Glasgow was named after it.

AND finally, the slogan invented by Saatchi & Saatchi as part of their £2,000,000 campaign to promote Glasgow's Year of Culture in 1990 did not go down too well with the populace; 'There's a Lot Glasgowing On in 1990' didn't quite take off.

The Diary put forward its own suggestion: 'See Glasgow? See Culture?', and asked readers to come up with their own ideas. These included:

Glasgow's Piles Better through Its Arts

Glesca – City of Culture an' That

See Glasgow and Die

1690-1990: We've Walked a Long Way

1990: Culture for Everyone – You Can Even Draw the Dole

Glesca 1990 – Happy Birthday, King Billy

Glesca 1990: Four Old Firm Games with Musical Interludes

Glasgow: City of Lally and Dalí

Gie It Laldy, Vivaldi

Who's Coming Out in 1990? Alfresco Glesco

Glasgow's Got Everything, But Be a Pert o' Glesca's Ert

The Cry Wis Where's Yir Culture Errzrafishulculchur

Culture's the Berries

What's Glesca Up To in 1990? Its Oxters in Culture, That's Whit

Glasgow's Hoachin' Wi' Culture

Glasgow's Full of It

Up Yours, Embra

Keelies Aye No. 1

Tiny Toi Dig the Bolshoi

Haud the Bus, Sibelius

Beethoven, Yer Tea's Oot

Glasgow 1990: Culture's the Biz, So
   It Is
If You Know Rennie Mackintosh
   from Rowantree McIntosh,
   Glasgow's for You

One last entry was: Culture's the
Jinkies, and came as part of a poem
which went:

> *What we think is*
> *Culture's the Jinkies*
> *We chow up culture*
> *Like a bloody vulture.*
> *We arra peepul.*

RELIGION

Over the years, the Diary has tried to maintain an even-handed approach to religion. We aspired to upset each sect equally . . .

THE wit and wisdom of Archbishop Thomas Winning: walking into an exhibition on St John Ogilvie at the Third Eye Centre, Glasgow, the archbishop was confronted by Pastor Jack Glass and a team of protesters, complete with an effigy of the Scottish martyr hanging from a gibbet. 'Nice day for it, Jack . . .' was the Winning remark.

LUIS Palau, the Argentinian evangelist, ran a five-week series of meetings in Glasgow in summer 1981. Like many well-dressed men of the world, the man of God with the presidential entourage and the film-star good looks made a pilgrimage to Ralph Slater's tailoring emporium.

Other customers were impressed by the way Mr Palau tested his four new suits for fit. As he tried on each jacket, he stretched his arms to the heavens and said: 'Yes, this will do fine.'

THIS story could equally well have

fitted into our section on Rabbie Burns . . .

The pope and Rabbie died at the same time and, due to an administrative mix-up, the poet went to Heaven while the pope went to Hell. After a few days, the mistake was noticed and a swap arranged. They met halfway and the pope said to the poet: 'I am about to fulfil my lifetime ambition, to meet the Virgin Mary.'

'I'm afraid you're too late,' said Rabbie, heading off to hotter climes.

THERE was a nun, we are assured, from the Sisters of Notre Dame whose ambition was to have her own car. After many years of saving, she managed to buy a Vauxhall Nova – and quickly became known as the Hatchback of Notre Dame.

A MINISTER and a priest were sitting together on the Glasgow-London Shuttle flight. The stewardess asked if they would like a drink. The minister ordered a whisky.

The priest, a vigorous abstainer, said: 'I would rather commit adultery!'

'I didn't know there was a choice,' the minister said to the stewardess.

THE suspension of Lord Mackay of Clashfern, the Lord Chancellor, by the Free Presbyterian Church because he had attended two Catholic funerals gave rise to some jokes at the expense of the FPs.

The FPs used to be known as The Seceders. One wit, thought to be from the Free Church, said: 'The FPs are no longer to be known as The Seceders. They're to be called The Suspenders.'

A second FP joke subsequently surfaced, a reference to their immaculate ministerial garb. What do you call a Free Presbyterian minister with one button of his black crombie coat undone? A poser.

Against all the odds a third FP joke appeared. It is the tale of an English tourist in Lewis who went for a walk one Sunday afternoon. He met a member of the local FP congregation on his way home from the service. 'I wonder if you could tell me where this road leads to?' he asked the local.

'If you're out walking for pleasure, it leads to Hell,' was the reply.

A follow-up joke had the English tourist protest that the Lord Jesus went walking on the Sabbath.

'That sort of behaviour might be all very well in Jerusalem,' the FP said, 'but not in Stornoway.'

Then there was the FP elder who died on a Sunday and went straight to Heaven where he berated St Peter with the words: 'And what are you doing working on the Sabbath?'

Finally, a definition of Free Presbyterianism: 'The uneasy feeling that some people, somewhere, are enjoying themselves.'

THIS tale concerns the many secessions that have plagued the Church of Scotland. The minister of a Highland parish is wakened at 2 a.m. by a ferocious banging at the door. He opens the door to find one of his parishioners. 'What's the problem?' he asks.

'Ah'm awfy worried, meenister,' says the parishioner.

'And why are you worried?' the minister asks.

'Ah'm awfy worried about the terrible schisms in the Kirk.'

'The terrible schisms in the Kirk?' asks the minister, beginning to spot that the member of his flock has had a drink or two. 'This is not the time to be worried about the terrible schisms in the Kirk. Come and see me tomorrow morning and we'll discuss the matter. But mind and come sober.'

'Ah cannae dae that, meenister. When ah'm sober ah couldnae care less aboot the terrible schisms in the Kirk.'

TRADITION, the Jewish version of Trivial Pursuit, contains the question:

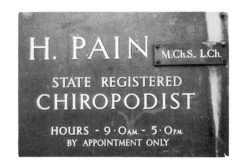

'Why do Jewish people always answer a question with another question?' Answer: 'Why not?'

Other, unofficial, Jewish Trivial Pursuit questions included:

Where did the Jewish kamikaze pilot land his plane? In his brother-in-law's scrapyard.

What is Jewish optimism? A Jew who makes a purchase from another Jew and hopes to sell it on to a Scotsman at a profit.

THE Catholic Church also had its own version of Trivial Pursuit, called Limbo, produced as a fund-raiser by a Canadian RC charity. It was described as 'an opportunity for everyday sinners to test their knowledge of Church doctrine, trivia, ceremony and liturgy'. The more po-faced RCs might disapprove of the rule which determines the order of play for a game of Limbo. The Tim who has been most recently to Confession gets first go.

SAYINGS AND DOINGS

A close cousin to Apocryphal Tales, Sayings and Doings is a category which allows the Diary to practise shameless plagiarism of other people's *bons mots* under the guise of claiming they provide a wry insight into society.

QUOTE from a public relations official at a Scottish New Town on being questioned by a news reporter: 'I'm sorry, I don't think I can be sufficiently vague on that one, so I'll just have to make no comment.'

ROD Hull, keeper of the infamous Emu, asked at a press conference to publicise his show at the Pavilion Theatre if his violent puppet had plans to wreak havoc on Glasgow, replied: 'I think someone already has.'

PROFESSOR J. L. Prattis of Carleton University, Ottawa, Canada, carried out a study into 'industrialisation and minority languages' on the Hebridean island of Lewis. One of the reasons the professor gave for the fact that Lewis folk had stuck to Gaelic was 'Isolation – this refers to the distance from interference by the dominant language group and can be operationalised in terms of geographic and communication criteria.' Or, to put it another way, Lewis is separated from the mainland by the Minch.

'BANK robbery is primarily an urban crime.' – Sociology lecturer at Strathclyde University.

'I WILL tell you why top civil servants are called mandarins. They are small, fruity, and give you the pip.' – Sir William Kerr, then Permanent Under-

Secretary of State at the Scottish Office.

A ROYAL visit to Glasgow by the Duke of Edinburgh progressed so smoothly that HRH found himself at the Pollok House estate 45 minutes ahead of schedule. There to greet him was Bailie John McQueenie, chairman of the civic amenities committee. Bailie McQueenie asked HRH if he would like to see round the Pollok House gardens.

'I don't want to detain you and your staff,' Phil replied.

'That's all right,' the Bailie said, 'my wife isn't expecting me home till half-past five.'

COMEDIAN Arnold Brown, now based in London, said he was appalled at the deprivation he had seen on his return to his native city of Glasgow: 'Did you know there is a waiting list of two years to vandalise a telephone box in Easterhouse?'

'ONLY a fool would attempt to predict the result of an Old Firm game. I think it will end up a scoring draw.' – Hughie Taylor, the legendary sports writer of the *Daily Record*.

PRESIDENT Reagan on his defence policy: 'First we get all the wagons in a circle . . .'

STRIKING miner with collecting can outside Celtic Park during the 1984 pit strike: 'Ian McGregor's an Orangeman! Support the miners!'

SIR Graham Hills, principal of Strathclyde University, said in an annual report: 'The consequential decoupling of the optimisation of our human resources from that of our salaries bill dispelled the prospect of financial disaster.' What he meant was that a number of staff had transferred to part-time work and the university did not have to enforce redundancies.

DOUGIE Lauder, from Nitshill, Glasgow, a contestant in a Pub Patter competition: 'Our family were so poor, we got our clothes in an Army surplus store. Okay, I know a lot of families did but how many of you went to school as a Japanese general?'

STREET trader selling bunches of green grapes outside Celtic Park: 'Eat the colours!'

THE Diary was invited to be a judge at a talent competition in the Casbah Bar as part of the Easterhouse Festival. The compère introducing the judging panel said: 'And this is Tom Shields, a famous journalist with the *Glasgow Herald*.' This was greeted with silence. 'The *Glasgow Herald*.' Still silence. 'You know, the newspaper. No' wan o' the wee yins. Wan o' thae big kind ye canny read in the toilet.'

A LADY, actually a deaconess of the Church of Scotland, replying to a particularly sexist Toast to the Lassies at a Burns Supper, opined that men were no longer as romantic as they were in Rabbie's day: 'I received an obscene phone call last week, and even he needed some prompting.'

COMMENT by a lady, one of a busload of Labour Party members arriving at a meeting of a Glasgow constituency about the time of the selection of a new candidate for the safe seat: 'Here, I thought we were going to the County Bingo.'

THE scarred relationship between police and the mining community took some time to heal after the picket-line battles of the miners' strike. At the 1985 Scottish Miners' Gala in Edinburgh, Mick McGahey, doing his MC, had to broadcast the fact that there was a lost child in the police tent. 'Could someone please go and get the child free immediately,' was how he put it.

ERIC Clarke, of the Scottish NUM, during a BBC Scotland interview maintained the trade union movement's proud record of mangling the English language. Asked to comment on the Labour Party's proposals on trade union reform, he replied it was 'good in parts, like the parson's nose'. The recording was stopped while a BBC person asked if he meant it was good in parts, like the curate's egg. Unabashed, Mr Clarke replied that he knew it had something to do with ministers.

A COMMENT from the newsletter of the Civil and Public Services Association, on the subject of a new staff assessment system: 'It's a vicious circle and it's the members who are at the sharp end.'

'PARASITE MARRIES SCROUNGER' – Heading from the *Socialist Worker* newspaper on the occasion of the marriage of Prince Andrew to Sarah Ferguson.

IN a greengrocers in Byres Road, a university lecturer is causing a small scene. In accordance with his anti-apartheid principles, he refuses the South African oranges he has been offered. The West End lady behind him in the queue chimes in: 'I do so agree. All those black fingers . . . '

A MALE colleague of a female journalist famous for her striking skin-tight jeans, worked up the courage to ask her: 'Tell me, how do you get into those jeans?'
   'You could try a couple of gin and

tonics for a start,' was the withering reply.

A ROOFTOP protest was in progress at Perth Prison. The men on the roof, not content with ripping off slates from the historic building, began to demolish the battlements. As the first chunk of masonry crashed into the prison yard, a member of the local press remarked: 'That's him in trouble now. This is a listed building and Perth Civic Trust will have him.'

OUT of the mouths of babes . . . A colleague of the Diary was attending a routine press conference at the site of the Glasgow Garden Festival. The occasion was the announcement of 18 jobs – YTS jobs – being created by Glasgow's parks deaprtment. The *Herald* reporter, interviewing one of the youths who had been wheeled out for the media, asked if he was into gardening. 'No, not really,' the boy replied. How did he end up in this job, then? the reporter continued. 'I got the job through my dad. He knows somebody in the masons,' the youth added, to the embarrassment of nearby officials. We presume the lad meant somebody in the stone-masons department at the council.

GRAFFITO on the wall of a toilet in Glasgow University: 'If President Reagan doesn't tell lies, why do they keep cutting bits off his nose?'

STRATHCLYDE Region re-advertisement for the post of Director of Water: 'The regional council wants to be certain that it has fully trawled the pool of talent at the highest level of water supply . . .'

No, we do not have any similar advert for the post of Director of Sewage.

THE Diary dates the turning point in Glasgow becoming a City of Culture to the Monday evening in April 1988 when the first performance of the *Mahabharata* was held at the Tramway Theatre. The London arts mob came north in droves for Peter Brook's nine-hour show. They came clutching picnic hampers, for which the Tramway had laid out tables. One chap was heard to utter: 'Virginia, grab a table. *Sans fumer* if possible.'

SAM McCluskie, the plain-spoken leader of the National Union of Seamen, speaking on radio about some aspect of a long and difficult pay dispute: 'I'll jump off that bridge when I come to it . . .'

THE three great weasel phrases are:
Your cheque's in the post;
Of course I love you; and
I promise I'll only put it in a wee bit.
An alternative third phrase suggested by the Diary was:
I'm from Strathclyde Region. I'm here to help you.

ASKED why there was no street in Dublin named after the Republic's first Prime Minister Eamon De Valera, an Irish political observer said: 'Well, you see, there's no street long enough, or narrow enough, or crooked enough.'

OVERHEARD on the Edinburgh Shuttle . . . Scottish Office minister Lord James Douglas-Hamilton chatting with a Civil Service minion: 'And where do you live?' The civil servant replied that he lived in a certain street in the New Town in Edinburgh. 'Very nice,' said Lord James, 'and where do you live at weekends?'

'PLEASE do not wander about during dinner and, gentlemen, please keep your jackets and ties on during dinner. Please sit down and do not talk during speeches. It is not only very bad manners but lets both you and the school down in front of the many guests attending. Please do not smoke until after the Loyal toast.'

Details from a letter by the chairman of Gordonstoun School Association to former pupils attending the 1988 annual dinner.

WHEN Rangers FC formed a professional basketball team, the captain, a Mr Jim Morrison, was invited to sample the Gers match-day hospitality in the Premier Club. He was heard to remark afterwards: 'A really nice place the Premier Club but I've never had so

many funny handshakes in my life.'

OVERHEARD in a Newton Mearns coffee shop, a lady is relating to her friends a rather nasty experience on a bus. 'This man sat down beside me. Then he put his hand up my skirt. You know the Jaeger one with the pleats . . .'

FROM a BP brochure explaining why they had decided to make more use of the colour green in their corporate identity: 'It not only differentiates BP from its rivals but if used in conjunction with certain styles creates a feeling of freshness, an impression of foliage, even of paradise.'

'MY wife can't stand the Scottish Liberals or Scotland and when she comes to power she'll see that they are soundly defeated.' – Denis Thatcher in South Africa in 1964, quoted by Ben Coutts in his autobiography *From Bothy to Ben.*

MINE host of down-to-earth Glasgow pub to chap who has ordered a Perrier: 'This is a pub, son. We don't sell watter.' The customer orders a gin and tonic and asks for a slice of lemon, to be told: 'Whit d'ye think this is, Malcolm Campbell's?'

HEARD on the touchline at a girls' football match at Inverclyde National Sports Training Centre: 'Go on, Amanda! Topple her!'

THE incredulous family of an 89-year-old bachelor who had announced his engagement to a young woman asked him two questions: Was it true? and Would he be moving house? His answers were: Yes. And yes, we want to be nearer the schools.

GREAT BOOK REVIEWS OF OUR TIME: A critic writing of the memoirs of Dr Henry Kissinger, eminent US statesman, said: 'I do not know whether Dr Kissinger is a great writer, but anyone who manages to finish this book is certainly a great reader.'

AN oft-repeated, but worth repeating, story is that when God was creating the British Isles he started with Scotland and was busy installing beautiful mountains, breathtaking glens, salmon-filled rivers and all the rest of the glories that are Scotia, when one of the angels asked Himself if perhaps He was not going over the top in the provision of amenities to Scotland. 'Perhaps,' He replied, 'but wait and see who they are getting as neighbours.'

A YOUNG lady in a Stirling hairdresser's, to her customer who was a musician in the Scottish National Orchestra: 'Are ye no' workin' the day?' Snip. Snip.
 'Well, I work mostly in the evenings.'
 Snip. Snip. 'Really? Whit is it ye dae?' Snip. Snip.
 'I'm a member of the SNO.'
 Snip. Snip. 'Och, I dinna ken onythin' aboot politics.' Snip. Snip.
 Update: Since then, perhaps in search of an identity, the SNO has changed its title to the Royal Scottish National Orchestra and then to the Royal Scottish Opera.

AS you would expect when a local legend is in hospital, Sydney Devine received special treatment when he was in the Western Infirmary, Glasgow, for a heart by-pass operation. This even extended to the nurses singing *Tiny Bubbles In Your Drip* as they wheeled Steak and Kidney into the operating theatre.

FROM the synopsis of *Glasvegas*, a musical play created for Mayfest 1989 by Borderline Theatre: 'Glasgow, where some are born great, some achieve greatness and some are still throwing spears at buses . . .'

AMERICAN lady in Edinburgh at Festival time, surveying hundreds of people queuing for tickets at the Tattoo office: 'Oh my goodness, look at all those people waiting to be tattooed.'

A HONEYMOON couple arrived at a hotel during a ceilidh. Play *Here Comes the Bride*, urged one of the dancers. The accordionist could not oblige. Play *Tonight's the Night*, was another suggestion. Again the musician knew not the tune. He eventually toasted the happy couple with a rendition of *The Muckin' o' Geordie's Byre*.

A MAN sitting at his wife's death-bed is asked: 'Hamish, grant me a last wish. Promise me you'll sit in the same car as my mother on the way to the crematorium.'

'OK, if it makes you happy,' he replies, 'but you know it will spoil the whole day for me.'

Then there is the tale of the man who could no longer put up with his mother-in-law. He went to the chemist and asked: 'Can I have some arsenic for my mother-in-law?'

'Do you have a prescription?' the chemist asked.

'No, but I've got a photograph.'

THE eminent cartoonist Malky

McCormick is also something of a philosopher. He presented these great imponderables of life to the Diary:

Why is there only one Monopolies Commission?

How do they get Teflon to stick to non-stick frying pans?

If Karen Carpenter had eaten Mama Cass's sandwiches, would they both still be singing today?

HOW do you make a zloty more valuable? You put four holes in it.

ON the familiar theme of rampant inflation we heard of the old chap who, on his way home from the pub, decided that a poke of chips would be just the thing.

'That'll be 45p,' said the girl behind the counter.

The old chap looked at the four florins and the single shilling in his hand and said: 'Nine bob? I can remember when you couldnae carry nine bob's worth o' chips, never mind eat them.'

THIS conversation was overheard on a Glasgow building site shortly after the release of Nelson Mandela:

'Jimmy's no' goin' tae South Africa.'

'Ah thought he was gonny be oan £10 an hour.'

'Aye, but they've let that Idi Amin oot and it's buggered up the whole thing.'

WHAT have you got if you're holding a hockey ball in one hand and a hockey ball in the other? The undivided attention of the Irish Prime Minister.

THE setting for this story is a bar in Glasgow's smart Princes Square shopping centre. A would-be man about town, well past his sell-by date, is attempting to make conversation with a young woman.

'Where do you work?' he asks, in an Oscar Wilde kind of way.

'Déjà Vu,' she replies.

'Is that a new shop?'

'No.'

'A restaurant?'

'No.'

'A bar?'

'No. Just the feeling I get when I'm speaking to you. I told you a fortnight ago. You've obviously forgotten. It was the night you said you'd phone me to arrange to go out for dinner and never did.'

WHAT with his Glasgow concert and his World Cup chart-topping single, Luciano Pavarotti became well established in Scotland's popular culture. Thus we reported a conversation overheard between a Glasgow mother and her young son in a seaside resort café: 'Ah've telt ye. There's nae f★★★★★★ Pavarotti oan the juke box.'

THE Glasgow Humanist Society calendar of events listed a meeting on Sunday, 16 December, at which they would have 'Yuletide refreshments' and watch the video of the *Life of Brian.*

TWO elderly women on the 57 bus in Glasgow. 'How's your man?' asks Betty.

'Deid – last Wednesday,' replies Sadie.

'Away tae hell,' says Betty, taken aback by this sad news.

'Aye,' says Sadie, 'last Wednesday.'

AN AA person warning Radio Clyde listeners about traffic jams, one day alerted drivers to a half-mile tailback at the Charing Cross underpants.

SIGNS

I was going to call this chapter 'Semiotics', but decided that was too pretentious and dangerous since I don't know what it means. Anyway, here is a collection of signs, small advertisements and other public notices which were brought to the attention of the Diary.

SIGN spotted on the wall of the hut which serves as an air terminal at Sanday, Orkney: 'Orkney Islands Council Emergency Procedures – Airfield manager, with assistants, cover engines with foam. Drag occupants out and clear of the aircraft, using hatchets if necessary, and apply medical attention.' Oh, and have a nice trip.

Spotted on the North Circular road in London, a road sign saying 'Golders Green 2 miles' and, added in neat script below, 'To you, 1½ miles.'

AN advertisement in the personal columns of the magazine *Country Landowner* indicated a down-to-earth kind of readership: 'Attractive, affectionate single lady, 35, having survived last winter in cold draughty inconvenient old home, seeks any unattached farmer with super new farmhouse. Send photo of farmhouse.'

From the small ads section of the *Cork Examiner*: 'For sale, gravestone. Would suit family called McCafferty.'

Small ad in *Oban Times*: 'Lifejacket, British naval standard size, near new. £16.50 – worth £25 (more if you're drowning).'

155

Coronary Care Unit, Inverclyde Hospital, Gourock. A special thanks to Dr. Turner for her constant attention.

FIRE. — The old pouffe which started the fire at 7 Douglas Cottages as reported last week, referred to an item of furniture and not the owner, Mr Donnie McArthur.

GENTLEMEN — Dunoon Speakers' Club guarantee you a warm

SEEN in Bridgeton, Glasgow, around the time of the Loyalist campaign against the Anglo-Irish agreement: 'Ulster Says No!' To which has been added: 'But the man from Del Monte says Yes and he's an Orangeman too.'

Heading in the *Catholic Herald*: 'Catholic MPs swing both ways on hanging vote.'

SIGN in toilet cubicles of C.R. Smith, the double-glazing firm: 'What are you doing sitting here when you could be out selling windows?'

A ROYAL Highland Fusilier sentry on duty in heavy rain at Edinburgh Castle was approached by an American tourist for the umpteenth time that day. The tourist pointed to the motto *Nemo me impune lacessit* carved into the castle entrance and asked: 'Soldier, can you tell me what that sign means?'

Sentry (wearily): 'That says "No four-tonners beyond this point", sir.'

HANRAHANS, a watering hole

adjacent to Glasgow Sheriff Court, commissioned an artist to create a spoof coat of arms. This was duly done, complete with motto *Quinque Lonicra Periclyneum et Piscis Prandium* which translates as 'Five Woodbine and a Fish Supper'. *Sic transit gloria mundi* . . .

A CAVEAT on a leaflet about the Cambridge Diet listed 'possible minor side effects'. These included 'headaches, halitosis, mild dizziness, constipation, diarrhoea, nausea, irritability and dryness of the skin'. Or you could also stay 'cheerfully chubby'.

THE sign announcing to travellers that they have arrived in the Kinross village of Crook of Devon had a piece of graffito added announcing that it had been twinned with the Thief of Baghdad.

A BUILDER'S sign in Kilmarnock was the subject of a few letters to the Diary. It read: 'The Poor Sisters of Nazareth New Sun Lounge Extension.'

FROM the *Dunoon Observer*: 'Fire – The old pouffe which started the fire at 7 Douglas Cottages as reported last week, referred to an item of furniture and not the owner, Mr Donnie McArthur.'

ERRATUM slip in the *Oxford Mini-*

dictionary of Spelling: 'The following error escaped our notice – for illitterate read illiterate.'

PROPERTY advert in the *Scotsman*: 'Set on the outskirts of this charming West Lothian village this exceptional detached Bungalow is set in ¼ acre mature gardens screened by established carnivorous hedging.'

FROM the minutes of Perth and Kinross District Council: 'Concern was expressed at dog fouling on footpaths and play areas and it was agreed to increase the number of hanging floral baskets next year.'

NOTICE in bar of Castlebay Hotel, Barra: 'Helen Whaite is our credit manager. If you want credit, go to Helen Whaite.'

AND finally, a piece of arcane graffito spotted in Glasgow's Maryhill Road . . . a list of youths' names followed by the statement: 'F★★★ the Polis and BBC1.'

SEX

This section on the subject of sex is necessarily short. The Diary never majored on sex. We have too many lady readers in Milngavie who might object.

SANDY Ferguson, for many years the urbane barman at the Rogano and Buttery oyster bars in Glasgow, told us he had only one dissatisfied customer in all that time: 'He was a chap who came in and had six oysters because he had heard of their aphrodisiac properties. He phoned later to complain that one of them hadn't worked.'

A YOUNG woman pushing a pram through Kelvingrove Park was engaged in conversation by an elderly lady. The old lady peered into the pram and said: 'That's a bonny wean ye've got there. And whit a grand heid o'

himself very well in his speech.

'I don't know how he managed,' she told him. 'He knows almost nothing about it. In fact, he's only tried it twice. The first time he was as sick as a dog and the second time his hat blew off.'

hair! Wis the faither rid-heided as well?'

'I don't know,' the young mother replied. 'He never took his bunnet aff.'

THIS is actually a tale about public speaking, but we don't have such a chapter. It's about a golf club where one of the social evenings involved putting slips of paper into the championship cup and asking each member to choose one. Most of the slips were blank but a dozen had a word or phrase written thereon and the tradition was that the member had to make a five-minute speech on that subject.

One member picked a piece of paper with the word 'sex' written on it. He proceeded to make a witty and knowledgeable speech on the subject. When he got home, his wife asked if he had had to make a speech. 'What was the subject?' she asked. Not wanting to go into detail, he said he had been called upon to speak about yachting. The next day, his wife met the club captain who said her husband had acquitted

AN advertisement on the notice-board of an arts centre in Edinburgh offered an intriguing service: 'The ultimate in intimate personal presents. Beautiful bronze life-cast sculptures. Phone for discreet, friendly sitting.' The gentleman artist providing this service was reluctant to be identified in case the wrong sort of people were attracted but he did say: 'What we offer is a fairly standard sculptural technique from which we can produce an exact replica of any part of the body. We do get the odd exotic demand.' The method involves dipping the relevant part into a plaster bed. A polyester model is then made from the mould and finished off in bronze.

The cost, at 1983 prices, of a sculpture you could truly call your own was £30 to £40, depending on specifications.

THIS is the story of a missed opportunity that could have raised awareness of the AIDS threat and made some welcome cash for Stathclyde Region.

Entire buses emblazoned with advertisements have become commonplace on our streets. Saatchi & Saatchi wanted to go one better on behalf of their clients, the London Rubber Company, manufacturers of Durex contraceptives. They wanted to use an entire underground train to get their message across. The whole length of the train was to be painted as a giant condom.

It was a project which would certainly have been eye-catching and potently symbolic. And the advertiser was willing to pay a lot of money – a figure of £1 million was mentioned. The agency approached the Strathclyde Passenger Transport Executive, who run the city Underground system on behalf of Strathclyde Region.

After careful consideration, the PTE bosses declined the opportunity to cash in on the world's first 100-foot mobile condom. The PTE has a strict code on advertising which prohibits messages of a political, religious or sexual nature. In these AIDS-conscious days, television, for instance, has abandoned its ban on condom advertisements. But the PTE could not bring themselves to allow the sight of a huge passenger-carrying condom slipping in and out of Glasgow's Underground tunnels.

The Diary suspects that the ladies of Hillhead and Kelvinside would agree with them.

AWAY FROM IT ALL

Editing the Diary column is mainly a solitary pursuit – opening piles of mail, answering numerous telephone calls, reading endless newspapers and magazines to keep abreast of world affairs. Occasionally, the editor lets you out of the office on an assignment that has already been turned down by everyone else including the office boy. Here are some examples:

SATURDAY: I have been told Butlin's is a different world. It is in fact a different planet, as I discover when I stay at their Ayr centre. Otherwise, why are so many of the guests wearing headbands complete with ping-pong balls on the end of springs, headwear apparently known as antennae? When at Butlin's . . .

Wearing my antennae, I report for tea in the dining-room. Why is waitress pouring coffee into my soup plate? It is in fact brown soup. 'At least that's what it purports to be,' says waitress. Butlin's have some very literate waitresses. Survive soup and rest of meal, which is very reminiscent of school dinners. Children want to go to beach. Gate to beach padlocked each night at 6 p.m. Beginning to feel trapped.

Go to cinema (entrance free). Film is *Escape to Victory* about Second World War prison camp. Still feeling trapped, leave cinema.

Take refuge from rain in building called Beachcomber Bar. Tropical setting very pleasant until thunder, lightning and rain start *inside* building. Don't worry, only special effects, says waitress. Order campari and soda and find, for some reason, Butlin's give large measure for price of single. Nice place, Butlin's.

SUNDAY: Raining. Head for church but diverted into adjacent showground, where all rides free. Queue at dodgems. Queue at roundabout which tilts at great speed and brings tears to your eyes.

Arrive late for service. Minister giving sermon on 'The first shall be last and the last shall be first'. He should tell that to the man in charge of the dodgems queue. Soup at lunch is red but tastes same as the brown. Lose in afternoon at table tennis to niece. Lose at pitch and putt, lose at bowls. Go back to showground and lose lunch on waltzers.

Children have joined Butlin's clubs (Beaver for age six to nine, 913 Club for older ones) and have a programme of activities that leaves them with approx. five minutes free time each day. Nice place, Butlin's.

MONDAY: Redcoat at breakfast urges us to clap for the sun. It rains. Lose to wife at table tennis. Lose lunchtime sweep at table on colour of soup. (I chose yellow but it is green.)

Catch brief glimpse of son at Paxo Rooster Rock show. Paxo Rooster is redcoat wearing chicken's head. (Amazing what they have to do for their £43 a week.) About 3,000 children doing something called Birdie Dance. Camp compère, very amusing chap called Gerry Griffin from Forfar, has theory that some parents don't come themselves but throw children over fence. Retreat to Beachcomber Bar which has moat over which children must not pass.

TUESDAY: Lose to wife again at table tennis. Get revenge by saying she has fair chance of winning Miss Whitbread competition to find 'cheerful, charming, and chubby' lady. On reflection, wife would have no chance in competition – it's full of confirmed Butlinites obviously weaned on years of three school dinners a day. Go along to talent competition but again would have no chance against Butlin regulars who just happen to have brought along dancing costumes, sheet music, guitars, saxophones, etc.

See son momentarily as he passes on overhead railway. Determined to win something. Repair to Beachcomber for camparis as fuel for Knobbly Knees contest. Too many camparis, too late to enter. Just as well as Gerry Griffin has contestants stripped to waist, kissing each other, and doing Tarzan calls.

WEDNESDAY: Challenge eight-year-old at table tennis and lose. Little know that he is Beaver Club ace player. Sun shines for Donkey Derby. Put money on number eight which immediately starts to cough and retch. Comes last after throwing child jockey.

Compère Griffin, parodying Butlin's tradition of applauding everything in sight, asks for a big clap for Tote board. We all applaud. Think I'm finally getting into spirit of things.

Catch son at evening meal (soup brown, by the way). Ask if he would like to play table tennis at which I know he is not good. Too busy, dad. Cinema, dodgems, pentathlon competition. Possibly spare some time Friday.

THURSDAY: No wigs . . . Lose at putting, lose soup sweepstake (it was red, not green). Spend most of day watching competitions. Glamorous Grandmothers ('No long dresses, trouser suits, wigs or hair pieces to be worn,' says brochure), all slim and obviously on self-catering. So many competitions, now getting confused. Is it Miss Lovely Hair or Miss Lovely Legs next? Or even Miss Lovely Hairy Legs? Anyway, lots of legs on display.

FRIDAY: Lose to son at table tennis but only by 22-20. Lose at snooker, putting. Despite school dinners, have lost half a stone in week. Celebrate with camparis in Beachcomber Bar. Wonder what volcano looks like close up. Prepare to wade through tropical lake (with plastic crocodiles) to find out but tall chap with green jacket and badge saying 'security' advises it is not good idea.

Join Paxo Rooster, 3,000 children doing Birdic Dance, and 43 redcoats in upstairs ballroom for farewell party till 1 a.m.

SATURDAY: Time to leave. Reunited with children. Buy antennae as presents for friends. Drive out of camp wondering how ever readjust to planet earth. Stop at perimeter fence for last look. Throw children over and drive off fast.

WHILST on a holiday bus tour of the French wine districts, far from Butlin's, the editor of the Diary was kind enough to send this postcard:

SUNDAY: Join bus at Gloucester Road bus station, London. Surely some mistake. Have booked (with four other ageing adolescent chums) for cosmopolitan, gourmet, connoisseur eight-day holiday of lifetime traversing France in luxury coach in company of other fun-seekers. Why sitting at back of boring ordinary bus? Why other passengers all grey-haired? Fernando the courier not exactly understanding. What expect for £160? Driving to Dover in thunderstorm. Overtaken by super-duper German bus with video, inside toilet, plush seats, disco, swimming pool, bar, restaurant and not a grey hair in sight. Lady in front of us is worrying about state of French toilets.

Reach France and Famous Five in back seat cheering up. Fernando makes announcement about 'bus rules'. Smokers must sit on right, non-smokers on left. Rota system for seats at front of bus. One of Famous Five (not me) now drinking litre of Martini by neck and decides to make own announcement. 'Will all people who are dead please sit on right hand side,' he says. Arrive Reims: chicken and chips for dinner. Lady who has still not been to toilet asks for cup of tea from wine waiter.

MONDAY: Early visit to Moet champagne factory in Epernay. Things looking up as find free bar. Fernando

165

approach and say: 'No, no. Visit cellars first, then free champagne.' Explain to Fernando only two things need to know about champagne. Is it properly chilled? Who paying? Lady still hasn't been to toilet. French ambience induced by Moet visit evaporates as Fernando arranges stop for lunch at a supermarket. If this is Safeway it must be Monday.

Arrive Beaune. More like Bo'ness on a wet Sunday. One of the connoisseurs has a bottle of Coke with his *boeuf bourguignon*. Dessert is a choc ice still in wrapper. One of Famous Five has had enough. 'Is this a restaurant or a cinema?' he shouts in reference to choc ice for pudding.

Escape from English fellow travellers to a little *boîte* called the Club Americain. Find only other people in it are Maurice, a property developer from Berkshire, his son (Maurice minor) and an architect from Stewarton. They are here to open Pickwick English pub.

TUESDAY: Day off from bus. Visit Dijon which is pleasantly full of French people. Real French meal in real French restaurant. Unfortunately lose balance and come to grief in one of those real French toilets. Know now why lady in bus has thing about French toilets.

WEDNESDAY: Eight-hour bus journey to Bordeaux ahead of us. Three of Famous Five do very un-British thing. Cut and run. Abandon bus and get train to Paris. French railways amazing. Book seats on high-speed train by computer from station. Immaculate buffet car serves smoked salmon salad, steaks, chilled white wine. British Rail could learn something here. Arrive Paris. Book into the Hôtel Opéra-Comique which name sums up the holiday so far.

Dinner at Boffinger's at the Place de la Bastille. Surprised to get in since one of remaining Famous Five (not me) is wearing jeans and a black semmit. Fixed menu at £10 starts with sea food platter size of a dustbin lid and gets even better the further you go through the card.

After dinner Terrible Trio (as we are now called) find ourselves at loose end in place called Pigalle. Nice Frenchman stops us and says the Piano Bar up the street is just the spot for nightcap. Place must have been some sort of health club since full of women wearing swimsuits and other casual clothes. Small bottle of Heineken lager costs 30 francs. Try to tell owner that he could get case of 24 bottles for that price in supermarket and brewery must be overcharging him. Lady in swimsuit approaches and asks will I buy her drink. At these prices can't buy myself drink. Will I buy her packet of ciga-rettes? Say I am surprised to hear mem-ber of health club is smoker. About to offer her some chewing gum when she leaves to talk to party of Germans just brought in by same chap we met in street.

THURSDAY: Lunch at a *brasserie* near the Gare du Nord. *Choucroute* and beer. Feel just like Inspector Maigret. Try to book seats on express train to London. Fully booked. Have to buy tickets for ordinary train. Thing is packed like bloody cattle train. French could learn a thing or two from British Rail. Take refuge in buffet where lash-ings of chilled wine and Perrier restore faith in French rail system.

Daunted by prospect of overnight stop in London which, as you know, is full of English. Get off train at Calais and find it full of English people. Visit made worthwhile by superb meal in Vietnamese restaurant which whets appetite for one which is promised to open in Glasgow later this year. (But will they make spicy pancake rolls like Mr Chung in Calais?) Evening stroll along main street. Hear sound of breaking glass from café. English hoo-ligans? No, *patron* and his wife have fal-len out and are throwing crockery at each other. V. entertaining.

FRIDAY: Would like to rejoin bus but can't remember itinerary. Train from London to Glasgow. Wondering if all worth money and effort. Scots soldier sitting opposite tells me he has got compassionate leave from his unit in Germany. Is travelling to Hampden to see his team, Rangers, in cup final. Takes all sorts to make world, *n'est-ce pas?*

THE LOBEY DOSSIER

ONE of the great highlights – but potentially the greatest disaster – of my career as a diary columnist was the great Lobey Dossier statue campaign.

Glasgow artist Calum Mackenzie came up with the concept of building a statue to the memory of Bud Neill, the cartoonist who entranced readers of the *Evening Times, Daily Record and Scottish Daily Express* in the

1950s, '60s and '70s. After the very first mention in the Diary of the plan, it became obvious that Bud Neill was a subject close to the heart of the people of Scotland.

The Diary ambitiously and perhaps foolishly agreed to organise the raising of the £10,000 which Calum estimated it would cost to raise the statue. The stookie is to be in the

form of Lobey Dosser and his faithful two-legged horse, El Fideldo. And this soon involved me in dealing with up to 500 letters a week containing contributions and answering scores of telephone calls. (As we go to press with this book, the Lobey Dosser Statue Fund is still, tantalisingly, £4,000 short of the £18,000 which the project will actually cost. And a year behind schedule.)

Fortunately, the letters which flooded the Diary contained, as well as cheques and postal orders, people's rich memories of Bud Neill and his work.

PROFESSOR Alan Alexander of Strathclyde Business School wrote: 'I hope my memory does not deceive me when I remember a Bud Neill cartoon of a barber cutting a customer's hair. I do not recall the caption, but among the small ads pinned to the mirror was a card reading "Budgies Repaired".

'There was a bored clippie in another cartoon, standing on the platform of her car saying: "Awfy quiet the day! Ah wish a cheeky wee man wid come oan wi' six dugs, smoke doonsterrs an' spit oan the flerr".'

ANOTHER memorable Bud Neill Glasgow clippie was captured for posterity, standing on the platform of her caur, all beads, bangles and war paint, singing:

'I dream of Jeannie wi' the light brown herr.
Wan inside and two up the sterr'.

JACK Weir, a Glasgow journalist, told how Bud used to give away ballpoint pens on which he had had printed 'Bud Neill – the funniest man since Rasputin'. Mr Weir's favourite Neill cartoon showed 'the man of the house standing in a doorway, clutching the good suit-trousers at the waist. Braces dangle from his outstretched palm and the caption reads: "Aw right. Who's took the knot oot ma galluses an' spylt the mechanics o' the hale device?".'

A simple, but side-splitting, caption accompanied a cartoon of doctor at a patient's bedside:

Doctor: 'Cumfy?'
Patient: 'Govan.'

ALISON McKenzie has a unique memento of Lobey Dosser, the Calton cowboy hero. Her father, Joe McKenzie, a journalist with the *Evening Times*, was a friend of Bud Neill, and he arranged for Bud to fill a page of her autograph book with a special drawing of the sheriff of Calton Creek. In the course of his duties, Joe also found himself backstage at the Glasgow Empire after a performance of the Roy Rogers show. Being a dutiful dad, he produced Alison's autograph book for an inscription by the singing cowboy.

170

Roy Rogers spotted the drawing of Lobey Dosser and was so intrigued to hear of the Glasgow cowboy that he wrote his message to Alison on the same page. Alison was pleased at the time, but over the years she has come to regret that her beloved drawing of Lobey has been defaced with the signatures of Roy, Trigger (actually, Roy wrote Trigger's name – the horse had difficulty holding a pen in its hoof) and Dale Evans.

SAM McKinlay, the former editor of the *Evening Times* who first spotted the talents of Bud Neill, has written from Woking in Surrey: 'Bud was a wonderful man. Quirky, touchy to a fault (his captions were inviolable), very, very amusing when he was in full cry, and with an unrivalled command of the Glasgow idiom.

'A percipient punter once said to him in Sammy Dow's [the *Times* pub]: "Aye, Bud, ye've a rerr lug for the patter." He was not only a gifted cartoonist and something of a comic genius with his choice of names for the Lobey Dosser series, but a shrewd observer of the local and national scene.

'I cherish a drawing of his which I felt ever since it appeared should have been reproduced regularly, rather in the way the *New Yorker* reproduces its famous cover every year on the anniversary of its first appearance. Bud's drawing was of three of his typical Glasgow wifies meeting on a street corner. The caption read: "Mrs Broon, this is Mrs Thomson. Mrs Thomson disney know whit the world's coming to, do ye Mrs Thomson?"

'I think of Bud every time I come across one of the many stupidities in our jumbled world.'

BUD Neill's surrealism was quoted by James Thomson of Glenrothes when he wrote to mention his favourite Neill cartoon. It showed a large lady, dressed in a peenie, hands on hips and clutching a scrubbing brush, standing in the doorway of a medieval castle with knights in armour galloping about in the background. She demands indignantly: 'Which wan o' youse galoots huz went an' slew a dragon a' ower ma clean doorstep?'

ERIC D. Clark of St Andrews recalled a pocket cartoon which would have been equally topical today. There had been reports of an operating theatre in a Glasgow hospital closed because of its dirty condition.

Neill had the surgeon asking for: 'Scalpel, forceps . . . wee brush and shovel.'

HOWEVER, while there was a huge response from people of a certain age who remembered and revered the works of Mr Neill, especially the Lobey cartoon strips, there were a number of younger people who asked who or what is Lobey Dosser and just who was this guy Bud Neill.

So, as a service, we provided about

171

20 things (well, 17 actually) you may or may not know about Bud Neill:

- Bud Neill was born in Glasgow in 1911.
- He may or may not have graduated from Glasgow School of Art.
- He was working as a bus driver just after the Second World War when he wrote an extremely cheeky letter to the *Glasgow Herald*. A smart cookie called Sam McKinlay, editor of the *Evening Times*, invited him to write for his newspaper. At this point, Bud Neill revealed that he also did wee drawings.
- Bud did a series of pawky pocket cartoons for the *Evening Times* before embarking in 1949 on the Lobey Dosser strip cartoon.
- Lobey Dosser was the sheriff of Calton Creek, a township in Arizona (pronounced Arizon-ey) populated entirely by emigré Glaswegians. His arch enemy was Rank Bajin, the accredited local villain, a man who had had the benefit of a public-school education.
- Bud Neill was no respecter of geography, which explains the presence in this Glaswegian cowboy saga of an African chieftain from Yoker.
- Also from Yoker in the Lobey Dosser strip was a character called Fairy Nuff, who wore tackety boots and who, in true pantomime-fairy tradition, spoke only

in verse. Her compatriots in the strip included Rid Skwerr, a Russian spy who had defected to the West and had been given a job by the Calton Creek district council as official haunter of the local cemetery, Big Chief Toffy Teeth and Pawnee Mary o' Argyll.

- Bud Neill wrote and drew 20 separate adventures of Lobey Dosser before becoming thoroughly sick of the character.
- Bud, in fact, killed off his hero in one of these episodes. He also had Rank Bajin reforming and becoming a good guy. But, at the end of the story, he told the readers that it had all been a dream. Whaur's your Bobby Ewing and Dallas noo?
- His ambition was to be a writer not a drawer. But, as the inventor of the keelie cartoon genre, he was drawn back to the Glasgow humour in his (unpublished) novel *Dan, Dan, the Lavatory Man*, based on the attendant in the public toilets in St Vincent Street, Glasgow.
- At the height of his career, Neill was a megastar, earning big bucks in the 1950s and 1960s. He was a snappy dresser – the first man in Glasgow to wear a zoot suit – and also favoured flashy, hand-painted silk ties.
- Bud was an accomplished player of the mouth organ. He entered a competition for harmonica players at the Pavilion before the war. Larry Adler was the judge

and declared Bud a clear winner. Mr Adler offered to fix Bud up with the job of moothie-player in Artie Shaw's band. But Bud preferred to stay in Glasgow, thank God.

- Bud had a pet crow called Ranky. He found Ranky stunned at the roadside in Stepps and adopted him. He rigged up a clothes pole as a perch for Ranky in the back seat of his V8 Pilot motor car. He also took Ranky into pubs where the crow would consume half-pints of beer. Bud himself consumed rather more than Ranky.

- Bud was the supreme Scottish pocket cartoonist, specialising in Glasgow bachles with shopping-bags. His words were even more telling than his pictures.

He wrote:

> *Winter's came, the snow has fell*
> *Wee Josie's nose is froze as well*
> *Wee Josie's frozen nose is skintit*
> *Winter's diabolic, intit?*

- Bud's technique when drawing a cartoon was 'to start with a neb'. This applied even when he was creating massive, full-colour works such as the *Battle of Bannockburn*.

- One of Bud's early creations was a Glasgow chap who was to be found hanging around street corners. He was called The Big Yin.

- Bud Neill died at the age of 59 in 1970.

Some correspondents felt that Rank Bajin, Lobey's arch enemy, did not receive the acclaim he deserved. The hooded, fedora'd villain, recalled one lady, had a precise, even scholarly, way with language. Once, urging on his steed (a conventional four-legged one) on some nefarious errand, Rank uttered the memorable threat: 'Forward at an increased pace, horse, or I shall have you painted by Matisse.'

BIG Chief Toffy Teeth was another favourite with readers of the Lobey Dosser cartoon strip. The chief had a way with words. Once, dealing with a revolt among the squaws of his tribe about discrimination against women on the matter of holiday entitlement, he settled the argument by explaining: 'None but the braves deserve the Fair.'

FROM the bottomless well of Bud Neill humour, Ramsay Armstrong of Forth, Lanarkshire, recalled a pocket cartoon in which a Neillian lady has her small son over her knee raising clouds of dust from his backside with the words: 'I'll teach you tae play peever wi' yer maw's tap set.'

A. TODD of West Kilbride brought back memories not only of Bud but of one of Glasgow's famous bakeries with a cartoon of the archetypal housewives clutching message-bags. One is saying: 'Peacocks is awfy good for functions so they are. If ah wis functionin' ah wid go there, so ah wid.'

THEN there was Bud Neill's poetry. Avril Stephens remembered (with the help of her aunt Betty Paterson, a Bud Neill *aficionado*) a typical verse from one of the Lobey Dosser strips:

I shot an arrow in the air
It landed I know not where.
I don't care
I've got mair up the stair.

A lesser-known but still beloved piece of Neill verse was entitled 'Spring':

The Snowdrop drips;
The crocus croaks;
And in my little windae box
A yelly daffy hings its heid –
It does indeed.
Oh, daff, could you but heid your
  hing,
Nae bother wad it be tae rhyme
Your heiding hing wi' Spring.

EVEN Bud Neill's fishmongers became involved in the reminiscences with some fond memories of the man. Hamish and Livvy Neill, distant relations of Bud, had an upmarket fishmonger's in Mitchell Street opposite

174

the old *Evening Times* building.

Bud would often pop in for a coffee and chat, usually when he should have been delivering cartoon strips to an increasingly anxious Dr Sam McKinlay, editor of the *Evening Times*.

To avoid the wrath of his editor, Bud would have the drawings delivered by one of the fishmongers. If he suspected that Dr Sam was particularly upset by late delivery of said drawings, a wee parcel of fish was often despatched as well.

HAMISH Neill tells that another of Bud Neill's diverse talents was that he was an excellent shot. 'He would bring rabbits into the shop. Normally, rabbits that had been shot would be blasted with shotgun pellets. Bud's were shot neatly through the head with a .22 rifle.'

AS somebody or other said: 'Bud was one of the immortals. It's a pity he's deid.'